Joan Baez

Consulting Editors

Rodolfo Cardona
professor of Spanish
and comparative literature,
Boston University

James Cockcroft
visiting professor of Latin American
and Caribbean studies,
State University of New York at Albany

Hispanics of Achievement

Joan Baez

Hedda Garza

Chelsea House Publishers
New York   Philadelphia

CHELSEA HOUSE PUBLISHERS

Editor-in-Chief: Remmel Nunn
Managing Editor: Karyn Gullen Browne
Copy Chief: Juliann Barbato
Picture Editor: Adrian G. Allen
Art Director: Maria Epes
Deputy Copy Chief: Mark Rifkin
Assistant Art Director: Noreen Romano
Manufacturing Manager: Gerald Levine
Systems Manager: Lindsey Ottman
Production Manager: Joseph Romano
Production Coordinator: Marie Claire Cebrián

Hispanics of Achievement
Senior Editor: John W. Selfridge

Staff for JOAN BAEZ
Copy Editor: Brian Sookram
Editorial Assistant: Martin Mooney
Picture Researcher: Lisa Kirchner
Cover Illustration: Vilma Ortiz

Thanks to Jorge Luis Firpi for his constant drive and support.

First Printing

1   3   5   7   9   8   6   4   2

Library of Congress Cataloging-in-Publication Data
Garza, Hedda
   Joan Baez/Hedda Garza
      p. cm.—(Hispanics of achievement)
   Includes bibliographical references and index.
   Summary: Presents the life and times of the folksinger who was a
major voice of the social upheaval of the 1960s.
   ISBN 0-7910-1233-6
         0-7910-1260-3 (pbk.)
   1. Baez, Joan. 2. Singers—United States—Biography. [1. Baez,
Joan. 2. Singers] I. Title II. Series
ML420.B114G37 1991
782.42162'13'0092—dc20   90-44108
MN   CIP
J [B]/Bae   119p   AC

Contents

Hispanics of Achievement

Oscar Arias Sánchez
Costa Rican president

Joan Baez
Mexican-American folksinger

Rubén Blades
Panamanian lawyer and entertainer

Jorge Luis Borges
Argentine writer

Juan Carlos
king of Spain

Pablo Casals
Spanish cellist and conductor

Miguel de Cervantes
Spanish writer

Cesar Chavez
Mexican-American labor leader

El Cid
Spanish military leader

Roberto Clemente
Puerto Rican baseball player

Plácido Domingo
Spanish singer

El Greco
Spanish artist

Gloria Estefan
Cuban-American singer

Gabriel García Márquez
Colombian writer

Raul Julia
Puerto Rican actor

Diego Maradona
Argentine soccer player

José Martí
Cuban revolutionary and poet

Rita Moreno
Puerto Rican singer and actress

Pablo Neruda
Chilean poet and diplomat

Antonia Novello
U.S. surgeon general

Octavio Paz
Mexican poet and critic

Javier Pérez de Cuéllar
Peruvian diplomat

Anthony Quinn
Mexican-American actor

Diego Rivera
Mexican artist

Antonio López de Santa Anna
Mexican general and politician

George Santayana
Spanish poet and philosopher

Junípero Serra
Spanish missionary and explorer

Lee Trevino
Mexican-American golfer

Pancho Villa
Mexican revolutionary

CHELSEA HOUSE PUBLISHERS

INTRODUCTION

Hispanics of Achievement

Rodolfo Cardona

The Spanish language and many other elements of Spanish culture are present in the United States today and have been since the country's earliest beginnings. Some of these elements have come directly from the Iberian Peninsula; others have come indirectly, by way of Mexico, the Caribbean basin, and the countries of Central and South America.

Spanish culture has influenced America in many subtle ways, and consequently many Americans remain relatively unaware of the extent of its impact. The vast majority of them recognize the influence of Spanish culture in America, but they often do not realize the great importance and long history of that influence. This is partly because Americans have tended to judge the Hispanic influence in the United States in statistical terms rather than to look closely at the ways in which individual Hispanics have profoundly affected American culture. For this reason, it is fitting that Americans obtain more than a passing acquaintance with the origins of these Spanish cultural elements and gain an understanding of how they have been woven into the fabric of American society.

It is well documented that Spanish seafarers were the first to explore and colonize many of the early territories of what is today called the United States of America. For this reason, students of geography discover Hispanic names all over the map of the United States. For instance, the Strait of Juan de Fuca was named after the Spanish explorer who first navigated the waters of the Pacific Northwest; the names of states such as Arizona (arid zone), Montana (mountain), Florida (thus named because it was reached on Easter Sunday, which in Spanish is called the feast of Pascua Florida), and California (named after a fictitious land in one of the first and probably the most popular among the Spanish novels of chivalry, *Amadis of Gaul*) are all derived from Spanish; and there are numerous mountains, rivers, canyons, towns, and cities with Spanish names throughout the United States.

Not only explorers but many other illustrious figures in Spanish history have helped define American culture. For example, the 13th-century king of Spain Alfonso X, also known as the Learned, may be unknown to the majority of Americans, but his work on the codification of Spanish law has greatly influenced the evolution of American law, particularly in the jurisdictions of the Southwest. For this contribution a statue of him stands in the rotunda of the Capitol in Washington, D.C. Likewise, the name Diego Rivera may be unfamiliar to most Americans, but this Mexican painter influenced many American artists whose paintings, commissioned during the Great Depression and the New Deal era of the 1930s, adorn the walls of government buildings throughout the United States. In recent years the contributions of Puerto Ricans, Mexicans, Mexican Americans (Chicanos), and Cubans in American cities such as Boston, Chicago, Los Angeles,

Miami, Minneapolis, New York, and San Antonio have been enormous.

The importance of the Spanish language in this vast cultural complex cannot be overstated. Spanish, after all, is second only to English as the most widely spoken of Western languages within the United States as well as in the entire world. The popularity of the Spanish language in America has a long history.

In addition to Spanish exploration of the New World, the great Spanish literary tradition served as a vehicle for bringing the language and culture to America. Interest in Spanish literature in America began when English immigrants brought with them translations of Spanish masterpieces of the Golden Age. As early as 1683, private libraries in Philadelphia and Boston contained copies of the first picaresque novel, *Lazarillo de Tormes*, translations of Francisco de Quevedo's *Los Sueños*, and copies of the immortal epic of reality and illusion *Don Quixote*, by the great Spanish writer Miguel de Cervantes. It would not be surprising if Cotton Mather, the arch-Puritan, read *Don Quixote* in its original Spanish, if only to enrich his vocabulary in preparation for his writing *La fe del cristiano en 24 artículos de la Institución de Cristo, enviada a los españoles para que abran sus ojos* (The Christian's Faith in 24 Articles of the Institution of Christ, Sent to the Spaniards to Open Their Eyes), published in Boston in 1699.

Over the years, Spanish authors and their works have had a vast influence on American literature—from Washington Irving, John Steinbeck, and Ernest Hemingway in the novel to Henry Wadsworth Longfellow and Archibald MacLeish in poetry. Such important American writers as James Fenimore Cooper, Edgar Allan Poe, Walt Whitman, Mark Twain, and Herman Melville all owe a sizable debt to the Spanish literary tradition. Some writers, such as Willa Cather and Maxwell Anderson, who explored Spanish themes they came into contact with in the American Southwest and Mexico, were influenced less directly but no less profoundly.

Important contributions to a knowledge of Spanish culture in the United States were also made by many lesser known individuals—teachers, publishers, historians, entrepreneurs, and others—with a love for Spanish culture. One of the most significant of these contributions was made by Abiel Smith, a Harvard College graduate of the class of 1764, when he bequeathed stock worth $20,000 to Harvard for the support of a professor of French and Spanish. By 1819 this endowment had produced enough income to appoint a professor, and the philologist and humanist George Ticknor became the first holder of the Abiel Smith Chair, which was the very first endowed Chair at Harvard University. Other illustrious holders of the Smith Chair would include the poets Henry Wadsworth Longfellow and James Russell Lowell.

A highly respected teacher and scholar, Ticknor was also a collector of Spanish books, and as such he made a very special contribution to America's knowledge of Spanish culture. He was instrumental in amassing for Harvard libraries one of the first and most impressive collections of Spanish books in the United States. He also had a valuable personal collection of Spanish books and manuscripts, which he bequeathed to the Boston Public Library.

With the creation of the Abiel Smith Chair, Spanish language and literature courses became part of the curriculum at Harvard, which also went on to become the first American university to offer graduate studies in Romance languages. Other colleges and universities throughout the United States gradually followed Harvard's example, and today Spanish language and culture may be studied at most American institutions of higher learning.

No discussion of the Spanish influence in the United States, however brief, would be complete without a mention of the Spanish influence on art. Important American artists such as John Singer Sargent, James A. M. Whistler, Thomas Eakins, and Mary Cassatt all explored Spanish subjects and experimented with Spanish techniques. Virtually every serious American artist living today has studied the work of the Spanish masters as well as the great 20th-century Spanish painters Salvador Dalí, Joan Miró, and Pablo Picasso.

‧ The most pervasive Spanish influence in America, however, has probably been in music. Compositions such as Leonard Bernstein's *West Side Story,* the Latinization of William Shakespeare's *Romeo and Juliet* set in New York's Puerto Rican quarter, and Aaron Copland's *Salon Mexico* are two obvious examples. In general, one can hear the influence of Latin rhythms—from tango to mambo, from guaracha to salsa—in virtually every form of American music.

This series of biographies, which Chelsea House has published under the general title HISPANICS OF ACHIEVEMENT, constitutes further recognition of—and a renewed effort to bring forth to the consciousness of America's young people—the contributions that Hispanic people have made not only in the United States but throughout the civilized world. The men and women who are featured in this series have attained a high level of accomplishment in their respective fields of endeavor and have made a permanent mark on American society.

The title of this series must be understood in its broadest possible sense: The term *Hispanics* is intended to include Spaniards, Spanish Americans, and individuals from many countries whose language and culture have either direct or indirect Spanish origins. The names of many of the people included in this series will be immediately familiar; others will be less recognizable. All, however, have attained recognition within their own countries, and often their fame has transcended their borders.

The series HISPANICS OF ACHIEVEMENT thus addresses the attainments and struggles of Hispanic people in the United States and seeks to tell the stories of individuals whose personal and professional lives in some way reflect the larger Hispanic experience. These stories are exemplary of what human beings can accomplish, often against daunting odds and by extraordinary personal sacrifice, where there is conviction and determination.

Fray Junípero Serra, the 18th-century Spanish Franciscan missionary, is one such individual. Although in very poor health, he devoted the last 15 years of his life to the foundation of missions throughout California—then a mostly unsettled expanse of land—in an effort to bring a better life to Native Americans through the cultivation of crafts and animal husbandry. An example from recent times, the Mexican-American labor leader Cesar Chavez has battled bitter opposition and made untold personal sacrifices in his effort to help poor agricultural workers who have been exploited for decades on farms throughout the Southwest.

The talent with which each one of these men and women may have been endowed required dedication and hard work to develop and become fully realized. Many of them have enjoyed rewards for their efforts during their own lifetime, whereas others have died poor and unrecognized. For some it took a long time to achieve their goals, for others success came at an early age, and for still others the struggle continues. All of them, however, stand out as people whose lives have made a difference, whose achievements we need to recognize today and should continue to honor in the future.

Joan Baez

*Joan Baez strums a guitar on the corner of Haight and Ashbury in
1967. The San Francisco street corner was the crossroads of the hippie
subculture and would draw thousands of young people to the area
during the turbulent 1960s.*

CHAPTER ONE

The Times They Are A-Changin'

On December 2, 1964, the normally bustling cafés and bookstores on Telegraph Avenue in the city of Berkeley, California, were quiet. In fact, as one looked up and down the streets around the University of California that day, Berkeley seemed like a ghost town. Shops and sidewalks were empty, and traffic was minimal. Everyone was at the rally. By noon, thousands of students had already started to congregate in front of Sproul Hall, the university's four-story administration building, to take part in the demonstration.

"Showdown!" read the leaflets that had been distributed and posted all over the Berkeley campus. "Come to the noon rally (Joan Baez will be there). Bring books, food, sleeping bags." Why were the students demonstrating? What did they want? Who was this person named Joan Baez? And why the sleeping bags?

The students had made no secret of their plans to stage a sit-in occupation of Sproul Hall, the culmination of three months of fruitless efforts to achieve their democratic goals. What they wanted was to be able to voice their opinions publicly, without fear of reprimand; to have a forum where they could express their views, however critical. Whether those views were critical of the actions or policies of individuals, the university, or the government should not matter, the students argued. What they wanted was the protection of a basic constitutional right—the right to freedom of speech.

In high school and college, students had learned about free speech and the precious Bill of Rights (the first 10 amendments to the U.S. Constitution). The United States, they were taught, was a nation where debate was encouraged, where people had the right to air their grievances and to petition, organize, and demonstrate for policy changes. Therefore, they had trouble accepting policies that limited the protection afforded by the Bill of Rights. The Free Speech Movement (FSM) emerged on the Berkeley campus and

More than 5,000 demonstrators, university supporters, and onlookers gather in University Plaza at the University of California, Berkeley, in 1964. Students staged a sit-in to protest the university's crackdown on student political activities and the exercise of free speech.

across America in an effort to restore to Americans the right to speak out on issues.

For years the Berkeley administration had taken steps to restrict the free exchange of ideas on the campus, and by 1964, those restrictions had grown tighter. In September, the dean's office had banned all campus political activities. There would be no tables, no free discussion of controversial issues, no recruiting or fund-raising for any cause whatsoever. Angry students had ignored the regulation and continued to set up their tables and to distribute leaflets anyway.

When 19-year-old Brian Turner set up a Student Nonviolent Coordinating Committee (SNCC) table loaded with literature on the movement for civil rights in the South, a campus official asked him, "Are you aware that you are in violation of the rule?" Turner folded up his table and left, but he returned in the morning, this time refusing to withdraw. His name was added to a growing list of "disobedient" students who were threatened with suspension and even expulsion.

Throughout the fall, a few activists continued to defy the ban on free speech, even setting up tables in the busy Sproul Plaza. On October 1, former student and community activist Jack Weinberg made an on-campus speech that explained why free speech also meant freedom to act.

> This is as much a part of a university education as anything else. We feel that we, as human beings first and students second, must take our stand on every vital issue which faces this nation, and in particular the vital issue of discrimination, of segregation, of poverty.

As students applauded, a police car drove up. Policemen jumped out, grabbed Weinberg, and shoved him into the back seat. Students rushed toward the car. Someone shouted, "Sit down!" and hundreds of onlookers did exactly that. For 32 hours, students blocked the path, preventing the car from moving.

Finally, the campus administration negotiated a temporary settlement, and the crowds dispersed. Weinberg was driven downtown
and released without charges. The eight leaders of the sit-in
received a disciplinary hearing, and a committee attempted to
negotiate new rules for campus political activity, but the ban on
free speech was not lifted, and the eight leaders were suspended.

Following the suspension of the eight student leaders,
thousands of students rallied every day at noon on the steps of
Sproul Hall. They agreed that the time had come to take bolder
action in their struggle for democracy.

That morning, Joan Baez left her home in the plush seaside
town of Carmel-by-the-Sea, almost 150 miles south of Berkeley.
With her teacher and friend Ira Sandperl, she headed north. She
knew that she was risking her shining musical career by taking part
in the controversial FSM rally. But this did not matter to Baez; she
believed strongly in the cause of free speech.

The career Baez was risking began in the late 1950s. During
those years, there was an international folk music scene. Some folk
albums even outsold those of popular recording stars such as Frank
Sinatra, Elvis Presley, and "Twist" favorite Chubby Checker.

Talent scout Albert Grossman was the first to discover Baez. He
spotted her performing at a Boston coffeehouse in 1959 and invited the shy 18-year-old singer to appear at his Chicago nightclub
for a sum seldom paid in those days—$200 a week.

She sang at Grossman's club for two weeks but did not enjoy
performing there. She could not tolerate the loud talking, eating,
and drinking that distracted her audience and drowned out her
music. She was a purist, devoted to traditional folk music performed without electronic amplification. The raucous chatter
made such performances extremely difficult.

The featured singer at the club, Bob Gibson, invited Baez to
appear with him at the first Newport Folk Festival, scheduled for
the weekend of July 11 and 12, 1959. For two days there would be
nothing but folk music and workshops in Freebody Park, a sprawl-

Baez onstage with folksinger Bob Gibson. Gibson, the featured singer at talent scout Albert Grossman's Chicago nightclub, later invited the young Baez to sing at the first Newport Folk Festival, held in July 1959.

ing green in the wealthy seaside resort city of Newport, Rhode Island.

Most of Newport's summer homeowners were sophisticates from Boston and New York. They made a sharp contrast to the 13,000 high school and college students who arrived for the folk festival in blue jeans and sandals and carrying sleeping bags. Many brought their own banjos and guitars. Baez was only one of several little-known singers slated to perform between acts. People had traveled long distances to hear the big folk names—Oscar Brand, Odetta, Jean Ritchie.

Trying to bolster her confidence and reduce her stage fright, Baez made a nearly fatal error by arriving at the festival in a black

Cadillac with her name emblazoned on its side. Folk music fans generally disapproved of any kind of flaunting of wealth. But when Baez walked onstage, her long black hair trailing down her back, earrings dangling from her ears, and sandals laced halfway up her legs, she won them over. Singing two spirituals with Gibson, her lovely soprano voice enveloped the spellbound crowd. Reporters flocked around her after the show.

The reviews showered her with praise: "Joan Baez is a phenomenon, a thoroughly natural yet polished and confident performer." They called her "the Barefoot Madonna" and "the Callas of folk song" (a reference to the world-renowned, dark-haired opera singer, Maria Callas). Robert Shelton, *New York Times* music critic, described her voice as "lustrous and rich as old gold . . . unwinding like a spool of satin."

In Boston, people stood in line outside Club 47 in Harvard Square to hear Baez sing her old English and Kentucky ballads. She toured the country, performing for full houses. Just months earlier, Baez had taken odd jobs to support her singing. Now she was able to support herself by singing, and there were many decisions to be made.

First there was the question of selecting a recording company. She had offers from a number of labels and the choice came down to two—Vanguard or Columbia. Vanguard was a small producer mostly of classical records that concentrated on quality and selectivity, whereas Columbia focused on quick profits and big-hit "gold records." The choice for Baez was obvious: She signed with Vanguard. Next, she had to have a manager. She decided to work with Boston-based Manny Greenhill, known for his efforts to get bookings for impoverished blues singers in the Deep South, instead of Albert Grossman, who offered her the "big time." Despite her shunning of commercialism, by Christmas, 1960, Baez's first record album soared to the number 3 spot on the 100 best-selling albums list. Soon her phone rang day and night with concert and recording offers.

Baez chose the Boston-based businessman Manny Greenhill to be her manager over Albert Grossman, who promised her the "big time." Greenhill, known for his efforts to get bookings for blues singers from the South, seemed more in tune with Baez's low-key approach to show business.

Despite the lure of dollars, Baez continued to turn down lucrative nightclub offers, preferring well-lit small halls, outdoor concerts, and college campuses, where audiences appreciated the soft ballads she sang. Baez refused to record more than one album each year, choosing quality over wealth. Her stage personality remained the same despite her sudden success. She refused to wear glittering gowns, high heels, or diamonds. She would not toss her mane of black hair flirtatiously or smile and wave coyly at her audiences as some suggested she ought. When there was wild applause, as there frequently was, she simply smiled, nodded, and went on singing.

The winds of change were blowing all over the country in the early 1960s, but particularly in the South, where segregation, or the separation of blacks and whites in public places, dominated every aspect of social and business life. Although the United States proclaimed itself the voice of freedom and democracy, it had been criticized around the world for its treatment of black Americans.

In response to world opinion, a landmark Supreme Court decision in 1954 outlawed segregation in public schools, unleashing an unprecedented wave of racial hatred in the legally segregated South. Inspired by the Court's decision, black Americans and their supporters began calling for equality on all fronts.

The Reverend Martin Luther King, Jr., with wife Coretta Scott King, holds a press conference on the steps of the Montgomery County courthouse in 1956. King and 92 other blacks stood trial for their part in the Montgomery Bus Boycott, a nonviolent protest against racial discrimination.

They demanded the right to eat and drink at whites-only lunch counters and water fountains; to sit anywhere on buses and in theaters and waiting rooms; to use the same public rest rooms as whites; to be allowed to vote; and some day even to have the same job and housing opportunities as white Americans. It did not seem like much to ask, but openly in the South and more discreetly in the North, people were ready to defend racial discrimination.

In Montgomery, Alabama, in late 1955, a courageous black seamstress, Rosa Parks, exhausted after a day's work, sat down in the all-white section of a city bus when the seats in the back—the area where black people were legally required to sit or stand—

were all filled. She was arrested, and the Montgomery Bus Boycott was born. For a year, the black people of Montgomery boycotted city buses, walking to work or joining car pools. Rich white women secretively arranged transportation for their striking black maids rather than do their own housework, while the city fathers jailed many of the leaders of the boycott.

Among the leaders was a 26-year-old black minister, Dr. Martin Luther King, Jr. A shotgun was fired through his front door and his home was bombed. Four black churches, where boycott supporters met, were bombed as well. But King persisted in leading America to a higher ground. His nonviolent approach became known around the country. "If we are arrested everyday, if we are exploited every day . . . don't ever let anyone pull you so low as to hate them," King intoned. "We must use the weapon of love."

Joan Baez agreed with King's nonviolent approach, and in 1962 she joined him at a banned civil rights march in Birmingham, Alabama. By lending her name to the civil rights movement, she was risking not only her career but also her life. Folk music lovers, or folkies as they are sometimes called, many of whom had been active in the movement themselves, applauded her commitment.

Baez continued to enjoy tremendous success. Her concerts sold out New York's Town Hall and the prestigious Carnegie Hall, and on its November 23 cover *Time* magazine featured an oil painting of her—barefooted and moody looking, holding her guitar. To have one's picture on the cover of *Time* was an honor usually reserved for statesmen and top celebrities. A six-page story lauded her musical abilities:

> Her voice is as clear as air in the autumn, a vibrant, strong, untrained and thrilling soprano. . . . No patter. No show business. . . . The purity of her voice suggests purity of approach. . . . It is haunting and plaintive.

In 1963, Baez returned to the South to join King again on another civil rights march to Alabama's state capitol in Montgomery. As she started up the steps of the capitol, wearing a jeweled cross around her neck, the police formed a phalanx to prevent her from going inside. On August 28, under the scorching sun at the Lincoln Memorial, in Washington, D.C., Baez sang the unofficial civil rights movement anthem, "We Shall Overcome." A quarter of a million people sang along with her, a highlight of the historic March on Washington. There King dramatically intoned, "I have a dream," and spoke eloquently of a future America where equality would be realized. By then, Baez's third album was out and her audiences had swelled (more than 20,000 people attended her Hollywood Bowl concert).

In November 1963, Joan Baez's name was in the news again when she scolded the president of the United States at a gala affair at the White House. President John F. Kennedy had been shot and killed on November 22 as the motorcade carrying him made its way through the streets of Dallas, Texas. Earlier, Kennedy had invited Baez to sing at a White House reception. A telegram informed her that the gala would still take place but it would be to honor the new president, Lyndon Baines Johnson. Opposed to Johnson's policies, Baez decided to attend anyway and do the unthinkable—confront the head of the nation in his own home.

Baez almost never made speeches introducing her songs, but at the White House she did. The crowd of tuxedo-clad men and bejeweled, mink-coated women knew little about a country somewhere in Southeast Asia called Vietnam, let alone that the United States was rapidly increasing its involvement in a civil war there. Looking straight into Johnson's eyes, Baez told the president that he should listen to the youth, that people wanted to stay out of the war in Vietnam. The evening had been filled with pop songs, jokes, and tinsel, but now Baez strummed on her guitar and started singing a different tune. Her choice was not an inoffensive ballad such as "Mary Hamilton" but a song composed by Bob Dylan— "The Times They Are A-Changin'."

The words rang out through the room with their unmistakable challenge: "Come mothers and fathers throughout the land/And don't criticize what you can't understand. . . . Your old road is rapidly aging/Please get out of the new one if you can't lend a hand/For the times they are a-changin'!"

There was a moment's hesitation and then, to Baez's surprise, wild applause. The audience insisted on the only encore of the night. Baez chose "Blowin' in the Wind," another song by Dylan.

A careworn U.S. president Lyndon Johnson chose not to run for a second term in 1968 as public outcry against U.S. involvement in the Vietnam War intensified. His successor, Richard Nixon, escalated the war despite the campaign promises to bring about peace, which helped the Republican get elected.

"Blowin' in the Wind" asked the plaintive and provocative questions, "How many roads must a man walk down, before you call him a man? . . . How many years can some people exist, before they're allowed to be free?"—a poignant plea for racial equality.

Later, local Democrats urged Baez to back Johnson's bid for election against the very conservative Republican candidate Barry Goldwater in the fall of 1964. They knew that if Baez added her name to the list of sponsors of the Johnson for President Committee, other young rebels might follow suit. But Baez disappointed them. She wrote to President Johnson, telling him that she would consider voting Democratic as soon as he "quit meddling around in Southeast Asia and brought home the troops."

At the rally on December 2, 1964, students gave passionate speeches. Then Baez took the microphone and sang "The Times They Are A-Changin'." She told the students to "muster up as much love as you can" and, as they all sang "We Shall Overcome," she led them up the steps and into Sproul Hall. *Time* magazine described the scene under the heading "To Prison with Love":

> Marching behind [Baez], who was wearing a jeweled crucifix
> . . . [they] stormed four-story Sproul Hall. . . . For 15 hours
> they camped in the corridors. . . . Stairwells became
> "freedom classrooms." An alcove was a kitchen. . . . For com-
> munication with the outside world, they used walkie-talkies.

Baez and her teacher and friend Ira Sandperl gave a class on nonviolence in one room, and then they wandered through the other rooms, playing songs and talking to students. By 2:00 A.M., most of the people at the sit-in were dozing on their coats or quietly reading. President Kerr was reluctant to call the police. There were too many faculty members supporting the students, including several who earlier in their lives had fled Europe because of Nazi aggression. Everyone agreed that it was unlikely that there would be arrests that night.

Baez and Sandperl left to make the long trip home and get some rest, but they had barely reached the parking lot when, on orders from California governor Pat Brown, 400 club-wielding policemen marched toward Sproul Hall. They ignored Baez and her companion; it would have been bad publicity to arrest them.

Inside Sproul Hall, the students went limp, as they had been instructed. For the next 13 hours, police dragged the young men one by one downstairs, bumping their heads as they went. They shoved the young women into elevators. Once outside, they packed everyone into waiting buses and carried them off to jail. Some students managed to escape by climbing out of windows or hiding, but more than 800 were seized. The campus reverberated with accusations of police brutality. By then, the majority of students supported the sit-in participants, and Kerr's authority barely existed.

A student strike was called for Friday, December 4. Many classes were cancelled by sympathetic professors, and others were half-empty. A desperate Kerr called for a university-wide meeting on Monday, December 7, and spent the weekend trying to win faculty support for a compromise proposal on student rights. But a group of teachers calling themselves the Committee of 200 met and drafted their own proposal supporting the FSM's demands.

At Kerr's mass meeting in the outdoor Greek Theatre, the president announced a new compromise that few considered satisfactory. As the meeting ended, Mario Savio, one of the student leaders, announced that the usual noon FSM rally would be held. Campus police roughly dragged him backstage. The crowd hooted and whistled. The next day, the faculty senate overwhelmingly voted its approval of the Committee of 200's proposals. In the corridor, FSM members applauded their teachers.

Kerr was furious. He now had to take the faculty proposals to the final authoritative body, the Regents. Most of them were wealthy conservative businesspeople, but the events at Berkeley

Mario Savio, a leader of the Free Speech Movement (FSM) at Berkeley, is dragged away by police at the University's Greek Theatre after trying to make a public statement on the issue of free speech. The incident followed an address by university president Clark Kerr in December 1964.

were a national scandal, and the Regents wanted a settlement. After all, at San Francisco State College rules much the same as those of the Committee of 200 were already in practice. Furthermore, lawyers had advised the Regents that if the FSM pushed its case in court, it would probably win.

On December 18, the impossible was achieved: The Regents agreed with a new liberalized set of rules for free speech at Berkeley. A handful of civil rights activists had set the stage for an explosion of campus activity throughout the country.

The song that Baez had sung that day on the steps of Sproul Hall—"The Times They Are A-Changin'"—had been prophetic. The spirit of the FSM would embrace the whole nation and help bring about the demise of two American presidents. Lyndon Johnson, faced with enormous opposition to his policies in Vietnam, would be forced to forgo running for a second term in 1968. A few years later, Richard Nixon would resign in shame on the brink of impeachment for his illegal acts against antiwar activists and others who criticized his policies. Millions would march—not only students but nuns and priests, teachers, laborers and professionals, Catholics, Jews, and Protestants.

The times were indeed "a-changin'," and Joan Baez would be there to "lend a hand."

Two-year-old Joan Baez. Before she was 10, her family moved from Staten Island to California to Ithaca, New York, and back to California. Baez believes that this constant moving contributed to the shy, withdrawn disposition she had as a child.

CHAPTER TWO

Vagabond Family

Joan Chandros Baez was born on January 9, 1941, in Staten Island, New York. She was the second of three daughters born to Albert and Joan Baez. Albert Baez grew up in Brooklyn, New York, brought there from Puebla, Mexico, by his Mexican father, a Methodist minister who had been assigned to work with Brooklyn's Hispanic community. A brilliant student, young Albert Baez excelled in mathematics and science. Originally planning to become a minister himself, he developed a fascination for physics at Drew University, in Madison, New Jersey.

Joan Baez's mother, Joan Bridge, was born in Edinburgh, Scotland. Bridge's deceased Episcopalian father had also been a minister. But there the resemblance between Baez's parents ended. Albert Baez was self-confident almost to the point of cockiness, whereas Joan Bridge's unhappy childhood had made her shy and nervous.

When Joan Bridge was only two, her mother died, and she and her older sister, Pauline, were raised by two abusive stepmothers in succession. When their father became ill and died suddenly, the girls were sent off separately to foster homes. Both of the orphaned Bridge sisters yearned for an escape—possibly into marriage and children of their own.

Joan Bridge first saw Albert Baez surrounded by giggling coeds at a dance at Drew. He was dark and handsome, with thick wavy black hair and a dazzling smile. When he winked in Bridge's direction, she blushed and fled. It was a year before she agreed to go out with him, but soon after that they were married.

On October 4, 1939, their first daughter, Pauline Thalia Baez, was born in Orange, New Jersey. A little more than one year later, Joan Chandros Baez was born. Albert Baez graduated from Drew, and he and his family moved to California. There he enrolled in a mathematics program at Stanford University and began to study for a master's degree. They lived in a small but comfortable house, the first of many. In the backyard, Baez's mother had a vegetable garden and there was a pet rabbit to feed. It was a brief period of happiness in a difficult childhood. "Springtime in my chest, and a lucky star on my forehead," Baez later remembered it.

When Joan was four, her sister Mimi Margarita was born. Finding the house too small for the family, Albert and Joan Baez signed on to live as houseparents at a local private school. Kindergarten was terrifying for young Joan. Whenever she was teased or the children played rough, she would have a terrible feeling of nausea. At night she was plagued by nightmares. Because the family lived at the school, it was easy for her to leave the classroom and run to her comforting mother.

Some 30 years later, Baez wrote, "Every year, with the first golden chill of fall or the first sudden darkness at supper time, I am stricken with a deadly melancholy, a sense of hopelessness and doom . . . whatever demons would haunt me for the rest of my life were busy at work even then."

It was not long before the family moved again. Baez's maternal aunt, Pauline Henderson, whom the children called Tía (Spanish for "aunt"), separated from her husband and came to California with her two teenaged children. She and the Baez family purchased a rambling house with many extra rooms and took in boarders to help pay expenses while Albert Baez studied for his Ph.D. One of the boarders, a cellist, practiced in his room while young Joan sat on the floor in the outer hall listening raptly.

The days at the boardinghouse lasted only two years before the family moved again, this time because of a new job opportunity for Albert Baez as a research physicist at Cornell University in Ithaca, New York. The Baez family moved to Clarence Center, a town of only 800. There young Baez first experienced racism.

Someone yelled, "Look at the niggers!" as the Baez family walked along the street near their house. Joan's mother and her two sisters were light-skinned, but Joan and her father were darker. The old man next door scowled whenever he saw Joan. But the family made light of the prejudice. They called their cranky, racist neighbor "Old Bogey," and Joan and her sisters played tricks on him. Still, for Joan, the knowledge that somehow her darker skin and black hair caused some people to dislike her filled her with confusion and doubt.

Again Joan adjusted to her new environment, making a few friends, taking piano lessons, and drawing pictures of Disney characters that her classmates bought for two cents each. It looked as though this time the Baez family would stay in one place for a while.

Albert Baez began working on secret military projects at Cornell. But soon he had doubts about doing research to develop war machinery. This was partly because he and his wife had become friendly with some Quakers. Quakers are strongly opposed to war and violence. Eventually Joan's parents became Quakers. Convinced that war research was immoral, Albert Baez left Cornell for a much lower paying career as a college professor.

As pacifists, Albert and Joan Baez were out of the mainstream in America. In the post–World War II cold war atmosphere, anyone who opposed the military was viewed with suspicion. The Soviet

Union, a communist country and America's ally in World War II against the German Nazis and the Japanese, had suddenly been cast in the role of enemy. The public was told that it was necessary to maintain and expand the huge armaments industry, employing millions of people to ward off the alleged communist threat. The House Un-American Activities Committee (HUAC) held hearings around the country to question people on their past and present political beliefs. Anyone who had ever signed a petition for racial justice or supported a strike ran the risk of being fired from their jobs and placed on a "blacklist," which in effect made it impossible to find other work. Even friends of those who were blacklisted were often charged with guilt by association.

For years, Albert Baez went from job to job, unable to secure a long-term teaching assignment. With each new job, his family relocated again. After leaving Cornell, they returned to the West Coast—to Redlands, California. A year later they left the United States for Iraq, where Albert Baez worked for the United Nations organization UNESCO, building a physics center at the University of Baghdad.

From the moment they arrived at the airport, 10-year-old Joan Baez was shocked as she watched a policeman chase a beggar, hitting him with a stick. The streets of Baghdad, Iraq's capital city, were worse. Legless children begged for money, and people rooted around in garbage pails for something to eat. It was in Iraq that Baez developed the strong conscience—a second "voice"—that would affect her entire life.

Joan and her two sisters attended a French Catholic school. There Joan's nightmares and nausea increased, and after only two weeks, her mother took her out of school. At home, happy to stay near her mother, Joan studied natural history, learned to bake, and made ink drawings for her father's colleagues.

All three girls contracted infectious hepatitis. Joan stayed in bed for months, certain that she was dying and afraid to mention it to her mother. Slowly, she recovered and ventured outside again.

Baez at the Royal Hunt Club, Baghdad, Iraq, in 1951. When her father, Albert Baez, a physics instructor, got a job with UNESCO at the University of Baghdad, he brought his family with him. The poverty and oppressive conditions that Baez witnessed in Iraq made a strong impression on her social conscience.

At the end of 1951, after one year in Baghdad, the Baez family returned to Redlands in time for Joan to start junior high school. The student body there was divided by an invisible color line— whites and Mexicans socialized separately. Being somewhere in the middle, Joan was excluded from both groups. Years later she told a *Redbook* reporter, "The white kids looked down upon me because I was part Mexican, and the Mexican kids didn't like me because I couldn't speak Spanish."

Joan's nausea returned, and as her 13th birthday approached, she thought of herself as "Joanie Boney, 15 pounds underweight, flat-chested, lines under her eyes." Unhappy and depressed at school, she used every available excuse to be sent home. One afternoon she left school and went to visit the Baez family doctor. He told her that she was beautiful and that when the other girls had "burned themselves out," she would be starting to show that she was someone "special." It was a turning point for her, "the beginning of the end of the sorrow . . . The work that had to be done to turn that skinny, frightened, ghost of a child into a real person would take years. . . . [I] made my own voice to be a part of that process."

For Joan, singing in the choir was about the only enjoyable activity in school. Her voice was still immature but sweet and true to pitch. When she auditioned for the girls' glee club and was rejected, she was convinced that her skin color had blocked her membership. But she did not give up. Instead she sang for hours in front of a mirror while she jiggled a finger up and down on her Adam's apple, trying to create a vibrato. A family friend taught her four basic chords on a ukulele, and she started playing and singing songs she heard on the radio.

When she thought she was ready, Joan took her ukulele to school and played requests during recess periods, even impersonating popular singers such as Elvis Presley. Emboldened by signs of friendliness among the other students, she entered the annual school talent show.

Her mother and father were there in the audience when Joan walked onstage, strummed her ukulele, and sang a top-40 hit, "Honey Love." The words to the song — "gonna get it when the day is done, gonna get it cause it's so much fun, gimme gimme honey love"—upset her parents, but both were proud when the audience asked for an encore. Baez did not win top honors that night, but in the audience many noted her talent.

Again, her hard-won acceptance was short-lived. The next summer, the family moved back to Stanford when Albert Baez accepted yet another teaching post. This time adjusting was easier than the last because Joan discovered that her musical talent was the key to instant popularity.

Joan Baez's social conscience first emerged when she was in the 11th grade at Palo Alto High School. She joined the Quakers' social action wing—the American Friends Service Committee—and journeyed with 300 other students to a 3-day conference at Asilomar, on the beaches of Monterey, California. There she heard Martin Luther King, Jr., speak. He told them about the Montgomery Bus Boycott and the nonviolent struggle for black equality in the South. Baez had learned about theories of nonviolence from the Quakers, but this was the first time she herself came in contact with a nonviolent movement. With the others, she cheered King.

During the next school year, Ira Sandperl, a bearded man with a shaved head and an odd laugh, came to talk to a group of young people at a Quaker high school, and Baez attended the session. He told the students about Mohandas Gandhi, the nonviolent leader of India's movement to gain independence from Great Britain. Sandperl impressed Baez as a man of feeling as well as intellect. Inspired by King and Sandperl, she decided to engage in a nonviolent action of her own.

Throughout the 1950s, the dawning of the nuclear age, schools held regular air raid drills. At some schools, when sirens screamed, the students had to crouch under their desks and protect their heads as the teacher yelled, "Duck and cover!" At Palo Alto High School, the students were instructed to leave quietly and call their parents to pick them up or hitch rides home. Once there, they were supposed to rehearse for an atomic or nuclear blast by taking refuge in the cellar. Baez knew that hiding under desks or in basements offered no safety from radioactive fallout.

One day while Baez was in French class, an air raid siren sounded. "I'm protesting this stupid air raid drill," she said, "because it's false and misleading. I'm staying in my seat." The local paper carried the story of her air raid refusal, putting her photograph on its front page. Letters to the editor warned that Palo Alto had "communists" in the schools. Baez's parents and Sandperl were proud of her.

As her confidence increased, Baez started dating, and by her senior year she had several boyfriends. If they started to get serious, she dropped them, not yet ready for love or a lover.

During her last year in high school, Baez once more experienced a period of nausea and depression, and her mother sent her to a psychiatrist. The counseling sessions helped some, and though her "demons" would never leave for good, she learned to deal with them. Singing was one of the best ways to drive them away.

Baez performs with folk legend Pete Seeger in 1961. Early in her career Baez was afflicted with terrible stage fright that brought on nausea and cramps. However, the symptoms always went away once she began singing.

Baez purchased an inexpensive guitar and taught herself new songs and chords by listening to the records of singers such as Harry Belafonte and Odetta. Tía told her about Pete Seeger, the most famous folksinger around, and she went with her sister Mimi to hear him perform.

Her first booking came from a teacher who had heard her sing at the Asilomar conference and paid her airfare to Sacramento to come perform. She even sang at a Shriner dance, where an old Shriner told her, "You've got a helluva voice kid. Don't sign cheap." She sang at her own senior prom, wearing a white evening gown, her bare feet sticking out from under it. As word of her talent spread, invitations rolled in, and Baez performed at other proms and clubs for parents of friends. Stage fright brought on bouts of nausea and cramps, but once onstage, she was fine.

Again Albert Baez shifted jobs—this time moving to Boston, to teach at the Massachusetts Institute of Technology. To please her family, Baez agreed to attend the Boston University School of Drama. On the trip cross-country, the car radio played music by the recording stars of a new folk revival—the Kingston Trio. Singing along with her family, Baez had no way of knowing that she would soon be riding on a second, larger crest of the folk wave. Her untrained but naturally beautiful voice would be her ticket to success.

For once the family was moving to the right place at the right time. The coffeehouses of Boston and Harvard Square would be Joan Baez's testing ground.

*Baez performs at Jordan Hall in Cambridge, Massachusetts, in 1961.
About this time she was ending her stormy relationship with Harvard
University student Michael New.*

CHAPTER THREE

Love Songs for Michael

Until the late 1940s, only a few people were folk music fans. Small recording companies sold a modest number of records by singers such as Pete Seeger, Odetta, and Josh White. Seeger had sung union songs and benefits for soldiers and war veterans. He treasured a World War II photograph showing himself as a young man, smiling, surrounded by soldiers, with Eleanor Roosevelt, wife of President Franklin Roosevelt, sitting in their midst. After the war, Pete Seeger and three other singers formed a group called the Weavers. Their version of "Goodnight Irene" skyrocketed to the number one spot on jukebox listings.

But in the spring of 1950, Seeger's name appeared in a book-length blacklist called "Red Channels: Communist Influence on Radio and Television." Employers were threatened with retaliation if they retained or hired any of the listed performers. At first the music world ridiculed the notion of so-called dangerous songs. But the irrational idea that folk music was something sinister, sung by communists in basements, spread quickly. Later, the same songs

The House Un-American Activities Committee opens its investigation into alleged communist infiltration of the entertainment business. Anyone refusing to testify was summarily blacklisted, or unofficially denied the opportunity to work because of suspected communist ties. Richard Nixon, then a congressman from California, is seated at the back table, second from right.

Seeger had sung to Eleanor Roosevelt and the troops were listed by HUAC as "gramophone records of seditious nature." A Weavers television series was cancelled, promised bookings disappeared, and the Weavers had to disband.

On August 14, 1955, HUAC began its hearings on "Communist infiltration of the entertainment industry" in New York City. The folkies made jokes about "overthrowing governments by force and violins," but for Seeger, subpoenaed to testify, it was no laughing matter. If he "confessed" and gave the committee the names of friends who had also signed petitions against lynching in the South or picketed for a union cause, he would be congratulated by HUAC and his career would continue—but his friends would be persecuted. Seeger called HUAC congressmen "the worst in America." Aware he could be jailed for contempt of Congress, he refused to testify, citing the First Amendment to the U.S. Constitution.

For two years Seeger awaited trial, singing the songs that upset HUAC and speaking out against the witch-hunt to small sympathetic audiences. It looked like folk music was dying, killed by the witch-hunt.

By the mid-1950s, youngsters raised in the atmosphere of bomb scares and the cold war made Elvis Presley and Buddy Holly their rock 'n' roll music heroes, rebelling against the conformity of the adult world with music that terrified many adults. In 1959, Elvis Presley was in the army and Buddy Holly died in an airplane crash. Rock 'n' roll had quieted down. The middle class danced the twist with Chubby Checker, and the airways carried the sounds of clean-cut crooners singing sugary pop music.

Buddy Holly, the bespectacled songster from Lubbock, Texas, became a rock 'n' roll icon with his hits "Peggy Sue" and "That'll Be the Day." After Holly's tragic death in 1959 at the age of 22, popular music for a time became a drone of sugary ballads sung by clean-cut boys and girls in varsity sweaters.

It was the Kingston Trio that started a national craze for folk music. The Trio stayed away from the social problem songs of Seeger and the gyrating hips of Presley. They wore tailored striped shirts and played to West Coast college audiences, singing sweet melodies in three-part harmony. Their records sold by the ton. Soon, similar groups such as the Chad Mitchell Trio, Brothers Four, and the Limelighters were selling millions of records, too. The record companies, dollar signs in their eyes, began forming and marketing more groups like these.

The "purist wing" of American folk music rejected the commercialism of these groups. The lovers of authentic folk music hated recordings that were heavily engineered in the studio. They believed that folk music should continue to be the music of ordinary people—unadorned, unorchestrated, raw.

In 1958, when the Baez family moved into their new home in Belmont, Massachusetts, they lived only a short drive away from Boston and the Harvard Square area of Cambridge. In storefronts called coffeehouses, students from Brandeis and Harvard Universities came to drink coffee, eat pastries, and listen to folksingers, jazz musicians, and readings by poets. For Baez, it was the right time and the right place. She hid her Kingston Trio albums at the bottom of her record stack.

Soon after their arrival in the Boston area, Albert Baez took his family to Tulla's Coffee Grinder, where folksingers and fans gathered. As someone strummed a guitar, Baez started singing in the background. Everyone stared, entranced with her lovely voice.

After that, Baez quickly lost interest in college. The music world in Harvard Square seemed so much more exciting. She spent most of her days at the Harvard Square apartment of a new friend, Margie, listening to folk music and learning new chords. She wanted two things more than anything else—to sing and to fall in love. Opportunities for both came quickly.

Sitting on the banks of the Charles River one day, singing and strumming her guitar, Baez saw a rowboat approaching. In the stern sat a young man with tangled blond curls. He listened to Baez sing and then rowed off. Infatuated with the young man, Baez searched for him all over Harvard Square, finally spotting him seated at a table with a friend in an all-night cafeteria. She stared at him through the window and he stared back. Baez walked around the block to muster up her courage,   but when she returned he was gone. After grilling his friend, she found out what she wanted to know. His name was Michael New; he was 19 years old, from a British family in Trinidad, in the West Indies; and he was studying at Harvard and spoke French. The friend arranged for New and Baez to meet again.

During the winter of her 18th birthday, Baez told her mother that she was in love and needed help with birth control, illegal in Massachusetts in those days. As usual, Baez's mother helped her out. The two young lovers spent most days at Margie's apartment; New barely went to class, and Baez dropped out completely.

The owners of Club Mt. Auburn 47, a jazz club in Harvard Square, planned to alternate jazz with folk and offered Baez $10 a night to sing. Quickly, word of a new talent spread, and two other coffeehouses booked her. For the next year, Baez perfected her playing and singing and began to cause a stir among the folk fans of Boston and Cambridge.

Problems soon surfaced between Baez and New. New hated the United States and dreamed of building a boat and sailing away to an island. The idea terrified Baez. Boats meant strange foods, seasickness, nausea, illness, perhaps even death. She was happy in the Harvard Square scene, riding around on a motorcycle, spending evenings performing. She envisioned herself as a troubadour and New as a rebel student. New's vision of the two of them alone at sea conflicted with Baez's growing popularity.

Baez recorded her first record in a basement with friends— "Folksingers 'Round Harvard Square." Then she decided to give her first solo concert at Club 47. New was agitated when posters of Baez appeared around the square. Success would corrupt her and

Baez performs at Club 47 in Cambridge, Massachusetts, in 1959. The club was the site of her first solo performance, and it was there that she attracted the attention of the major figures of the folk movement. Her pay was $10 a night.

she would lose him, he warned. The idea of losing him terrified her, but Baez refused to give up her music.

In the spring, Baez went to work—the first of the only two nonsinging jobs she would ever hold. She gave motor scooter lessons for $1.25 per hour. Just as she was "going crazy from people who had no sense of balance," Albert Grossman offered her the chance to sing at the Gate of Horn in Chicago.

New was visiting his family in Trinidad when Baez catapulted to fame at the 1959 Newport Folk Festival. When he returned, Baez the little-known itinerant folksinger had become Joan Baez the enchanting Barefoot Madonna. Invitations poured in, and Baez accepted them, singing in Greenwich Village, at the University of Massachusetts summer concerts, even joining Pete Seeger for a concert. Club 47 raised her pay to $25 a night.

Somehow she sandwiched in another job—working during the day with kindergarten children as a housemother at Perkins Institute for the Blind. The punishments doled out at the institute upset the young singer, but the school administrators were not interested in Baez's educational philosophy. After two months they discharged her. The official reason was her bohemian style of dressing and bare feet.

In the summer of 1960, while New visited Trinidad again, Baez went to New York to record her first Vanguard album. Her parents were heading back to California, and for the first time Baez was completely on her own. She and an old high school friend rented a tiny apartment. When Michael New returned, they were sometimes happy together, but at other times they were not.

Baez gave her first solo performance in New York City at the prestigious 92nd Street Y, in an 800-seat auditorium overflowing with fans. The more invitations to sing she received, the meaner New became, until they actually came to blows. Baez, advocate of nonviolence, found herself throwing things around the apartment, kicking New and pulling his hair. New convinced Baez that the only way they could stay together was to leave the East Coast and go to California, where there were fewer opportunities for folk musicians. Her manager, Manny Greenhill, wept, but Baez promised she would come east for concerts.

Baez's first record was released around Christmas and soared to the number three spot in the nation. New's bitterness increased. Not only was he jealous of her career, but he also thought that her nonviolent philosophy was silly nonsense.

In 1961, Baez commuted back and forth to the East Coast to give 20 concerts, including a standing-room-only event that filled Town Hall in New York. When Coca-Cola offered her $50,000 to do an advertisement, Baez flatly rejected the idea. "I don't want to become a product," she told an interviewer.

Baez and New moved to a $35-a-month cabin in Big Sur, a lovely wild spot surrounded by the roaring Pacific on one side and stately redwood trees on the other. They bought a silver Jaguar XKE and for kicks drove it at dangerously high speeds along the curvy coastal precipices.

The time for a decision about their relationship was drawing closer, but Baez did not yet have the courage to tell New she was leaving him. They left for a vacation in Mexico. Baez was ill during the entire trip. When she returned, she posed for a cover portrait for *Time* and then checked into a hospital. She weighed 102 pounds and was diagnosed as malnourished, dehydrated, and riddled with gastrointestinal and pulmonary viruses. To make matters worse, New behaved as though her illness was imaginary. For the first time, Baez felt only rage toward him.

While in the hospital, Baez received a note from a 17-year-old girl named Kim who wanted to visit her, offering to wash her car for her. Baez invited Kim to the hospital, and the two quickly became close friends.

Home from the hospital, Baez received an incredible plum for her career—a chance to appear on the new ABC television folk music show "Hootenanny." But ABC's invitation presented her with a difficult choice of conscience. Pete Seeger, whose "freedom of song" case had finally come up for trial, had been banned from the show. Found guilty of contempt of Congress, Seeger was given a 10-year sentence that he appealed. On March 31, 1961, the *New York Post* said about Seeger's ordeal, "Some jail will be a more joyous place if he lands there, and things will be bleaker on the outside." In May, the court of appeals ruled in favor of Seeger on the technicality of a faulty indictment, sidestepping the issue of freedom to sing.

The "Hootenanny" producers never told Seeger that they were banning him from the show, but the word leaked out. As much as

Baez longed to make her television debut, she joined with 49 other singers and formed the Hootenanny Boycott Committee, carrying picket signs with End the Blacklist printed on them outside ABC's Manhattan studios. The "Hootenanny" producers relented slightly: Pete Seeger could appear on their program if he signed a loyalty oath.

"Dear ABC," Seeger responded, "I just finished a seven-year court battle to prove the principle that such oaths are unconstitutional, and I was acquitted and vindicated." "Hootenanny" never answered.

Baez forgot about television and toured the East Coast with Seeger. In New York, they were cheered by an overflow crowd at Carnegie Hall. That evening, Baez wrote a farewell letter to Michael New. When she finished she felt "light as silk."

Home in California, Baez rented a cottage. Kim came to visit, and Baez offered her a room. Gradually a secret love affair developed between the two women. They rented a house in the Carmel highlands while Baez's new house in the valley was being built. They broke up when Baez started going out with men and Kim tried to stop her. New had tried to control her, and Baez had no intention of remaining in another unhappy situation.

Almost a decade later, a reporter asked Baez about her sexual preferences. Baez responded, "I had an affair with a girl when I was [in my early twenties]. It was wonderful. . . . I have not had another affair with a woman [since] nor the conscious desire to."

However deep her love had been for Michael and for Kim, the world media would become much more excited about her next romance. Bob Dylan was about to rekindle her passions, and the Vietnam War her social conscience.

Baez leads a civil rights protest in 1964 at the University of Texas at Austin. The civil rights movement was but one of many causes to which the folksinger would lend her name and music throughout her career.

CHAPTER FOUR

Diamonds and Rust

In 1961, New York City's Greenwich Village was the center for a new generation of political songwriters and singers. Enthusiastic audiences flocked to music spots such as Gerde's Folk City on West Fourth Street, where Phil Ochs, Tom Paxton, and dozens of others wrote and sang topical songs.

Just as Baez's arrival in Boston had coincided with the folk music revival, Bob Dylan's first appearance at Folk City in April 1961 came at the perfect time for his unusual brand of protest music. Village folkies were impressed by Dylan's original songs. His hoarse voice and mysterious past gave him a certain charisma.

It was at Folk City that Baez met Dylan for the first time. She was seated with Michael New and her sister Mimi when Dylan was introduced to them. Although she thought that his nasal tones and scruffy appearance would work against him, Baez later recollected, "he really made me happy that there was somebody with that kind of talent." But she could not pay much attention to Dylan with New acting like his usual jealous self. Dylan stood ill at ease in Baez's presence. Both of them were 20, but Baez felt "like the old dowager of the folk scene."

Shortly after he showed up at Folk City, Dylan met 17-year-old Suze Rotolo, who lived in the Village with her sister Carla. Rotolo introduced him to Bertolt Brecht's poetry, which became a strong influence on his songwriting.

With the help of other new friends, Dylan was invited to sing at Cambridge's Club 47. But the purist audience that had listened so spellbound to Baez found Dylan's music too experimental. He returned to Suze and Carla Rotolo's Greenwich Village apartment disillusioned. Later, Dylan and Suze Rotolo moved into an apartment of their own on West Fourth Street.

In the summer of 1962, through Suze Rotolo's connections, Dylan was invited to sing at a fund-raiser at Carnegie Hall for the civil rights movement. Notables such as Baez and Seeger also performed. Rumors of a Baez-Dylan romance soon reached Rotolo's ears, but Dylan claimed that he did not like the "queen of folk" or the weepy ballads she sang. Dylan's music began to attract considerable attention, especially his "Hard Rain's A-Gonna Fall," a song about the dangers of nuclear war.

During that summer of 1962, Baez was touring black colleges in the South with Manny Greenhill and Kim. In Birmingham, Alabama, they checked in at the Gadston Motel, the only integrated motel in town, where Dr. Martin Luther King, Jr., and his entourage were also staying. There Baez met King for the second time. The next day as Baez sang at nearby Miles College, there were mass arrests, and the Gadston Motel was bombed.

Greenhill had brought along a prerelease copy of Dylan's forthcoming album, *The Freewheelin' Bob Dylan.* Baez was impressed by the powerful lyrics about war, peace, and the bomb. She decided to take a longer look at the musician and his music.

In May 1963, Baez went to hear Dylan sing at the Monterey Folk Festival in California. After the concert, the "queen of folk" rushed up to Dylan. She longed to learn his songs, but other longings were involved, too. They eventually ended up at Baez's home in Carmel, where for several weeks Dylan played and Baez listened. Though Dylan called Rotolo frequently from Baez's house, by the time Dylan returned to the East Coast, he and Baez had become lovers and had agreed that he would accompany her on her next tour and perform as her surprise guest. It would be a chance to display his talents to a much wider audience.

Soon after the 1963 Monterey festival, Baez was interviewed by journalist Nat Hentoff for *HiFi/Stereo Review* magazine. When asked about Dylan, she said the following:

> The majority of those "protest" songs are stupid. They're
> without beauty. By contrast, Bob Dylan's songs . . . are power-
> ful as poetry and. . . as music. . . . Bob is expressing what
> all these kids want to say. And I love his singing! Oh, my God,
> the boy can sing! He can be so terribly moving. I've never
> heard anyone like him. When he starts singing . . . "Hard
> Rain," I cry and have to leave the room.

At the end of May 1963, *The Freewheelin' Bob Dylan* was officially released. On its cover was a photograph of Dylan and Suze Rotolo, walking down a windblown Greenwich Village street, Rotolo's cheek pressed against Dylan's shoulder. John Sebastian, founder of the group the Lovin' Spoonful, once said of Dylan, "You can't get too close to [him]. He burns with such a bright flame you can get burned." Baez would learn this lesson the hard way.

By early July, civil rights workers were familiar with Dylan's protest songs. They invited him to a rally in Greenwood, Mississippi, where a voter registration drive was in progress. Dylan sang his new song, "Only a Pawn in Their Game," about the murdered civil rights worker Medgar Evers. It would become one of the most memorable songs of the struggle.

That month, Dylan was invited to perform at the Newport Folk Festival. He accepted the invitation and arrived with Suze Rotolo. A number of the performers at the festival sang Dylan songs, and

Baez and Bob Dylan onstage at the Newport Folk Festival in 1963. Baez was struck by his scratchy, nasal voice, his unpretentious clothes, and his powerful lyrics. When Baez asked Dylan to join her onstage at Newport, their stormy relationship began.

Pete Seeger praised him from the stage. The audience loved Dylan's unpretentious clothing and his scratchy voice, so different from the usual sweet lilting style of the traditional folksingers. Most of all they went wild over his biting verses. Reporters and fans followed him. It was like a repeat of Baez's experience in 1959. Dylan left Newport a star.

At the last concert of the festival, Baez performed several of Dylan's songs and then announced, "Here's another Bobby song.

This is a song about a love affair that has lasted too long," before singing "Don't Think Twice, It's All Right." Rotolo blanched. Baez then called Dylan to the stage, and they combined for a rendition of "With God on Our Side." The crowd went wild. Dylan instantly was made the reigning prince at the side of the queen of folk. Suze Rotolo, shaken, left the grounds.

Sometime that weekend, Baez told Dylan that her tour with him had finally been arranged. After he told Rotolo about it, Dylan came home the next day to find her on the floor, the oven gas turned on. Rotolo recovered from her suicide attempt and moved in with her sister Carla. Dylan made no effort to woo her back; he and Baez were a team. At the March on Washington, August 28, 1963, they sang duets to a crowd of 250,000 at the Lincoln Memorial. He was making his third album, *The Times They Are A-Changin'.*

By then, the whole world suspected that there was more than just music between Dylan and Baez. They still lived on opposite coasts, however, and Dylan, alone in New York, began to suffer from loneliness and the effects of his newfound success. Baez always became nauseous under stress, but Dylan, chased by fans, became surly, paranoid, mean-spirited. Feeling the pressure, he again sought out Suze Rotolo. Despite Carla Rotolo's efforts to stop her sister from consenting, Dylan moved in with them.

That fall, Suze Rotolo learned that she was pregnant. Dylan convinced Bob Grossman to arrange for an abortion—illegal until the early 1970s. For days after the operation, Rotolo hemorrhaged, afraid to go to a hospital for fear that she would get others in trouble. When she recovered, she broke with Dylan for good.

Baez and Dylan became the darlings of the folk-rock world—the king and queen—openly in love, written about by every gossip columnist in the country. But things were never the same again after those happy days in New York. Dylan's moody, secretive ways conflicted with Baez's natural openness and honesty. He became involved in an affair with model Sara Lowndes.

Meanwhile, the civil rights movement was gaining momentum in the United States despite violent resistance. Thousands of black demonstrators faced snarling police dogs, torrents of water from fire hoses, tear gas, and police beatings. The notorious Ku Klux Klan (KKK) and their many supporters in the police and the FBI were determined to fight the movement. The KKK was a secret organization that used violence against anyone daring to advocate equality among the races. Its members burned crosses on lawns and assaulted and sometimes even killed people to defend its notions of

A burning cross illuminates the hooded figures of the Ku Klux Klan. The KKK, often with the support of local police forces, resisted the movement for black equality in the South with beatings, fire hoses, attack dogs, and frequently murder.

white supremacy. For decades, Klansmen, who wore white pointy hooded sheets with only their eyes exposed, had terrorized black people.

The violence intensified during the mid-1960s. Four young girls were killed when a bomb exploded in the midst of their Sunday school class in a black church in Birmingham. Scores of other churches were bombed, and many volunteers were severely beaten. The bodies of three young SNCC workers—James Chaney, a black Mississippian, and two white Jewish volunteers from the north were found brutally beaten to death and buried in a swamp.

This violence, which they witnessed each night on the television news, forced people to look at segregation in their own backyard and to examine their own feelings. Elsewhere in the nation discrimination was not enforced by law as it was in the South, but it existed nonetheless. Everyone knew that all over the United States black people had long been denied basic human rights and were forced to live in segregated slum housing and to attend inferior segregated schools.

During this tumultuous period, politicians and businessmen pressured the University of California administration to put a stop to campus organizing, particularly on the Berkeley campus where civil rights demonstrations were becoming frequent. University president Clark Kerr complied in September 1964 by banning campus political activity. The FSM sit-in ensued as defiant Berkeley students organized and demanded their rights. Baez came to Berkeley many times to lead the singing of civil rights and union songs, attracting publicity for the FSM.

After Lyndon Johnson's election as president of the United States, Baez decided to refuse to pay the military portion of her taxes. Her widely published letter to the Internal Revenue Service said: "I am not going to volunteer the 60 percent of my year's income tax that goes to armaments. . . . Now we plan and build weapons that can take thousands of lives in a second, millions of

The Beatles (from left: George Harrison, John Lennon, Paul McCartney, and Ringo Starr) took America by storm in 1964. The Fab Four appeared several times on the "Ed Sullivan Show" and played to a packed Shea Stadium in New York. Their sound changed popular music forever and remains an influence to this day.

lives in a day, billions in a week. . . . So all I can do is draw my own line now."

The IRS put a lien on her house, car, and land. Treasury agents arrived at the box offices of halls where Baez was performing to claim back taxes from her receipts. Baez had not taken the action to save money. She hoped that she would be the harbinger of a tax resistance movement against the Vietnam War.

In the meantime, Baez toured with Dylan to rave reviews. On tour, they met the mop-top British pop group the Beatles, who were then storming the charts with such hits as "Please Please Me" and "She Loves You." America was beginning to fall under the spell of

Beatlemania, and Dylan and Baez were happy to meet the Fab Four—John, Paul, George, and Ringo—who had brought the Mersey sound of working-class England from their hometown of Liverpool to the United States. Dylan and Baez spent an evening with the Beatles, laughing and singing songs until 3:00 A.M.

During the tour, grim news came from Selma, Alabama. More than 1,000 of Martin Luther King's followers had been thrown in jail. Also, Jimmie Lee Jackson, a young voter registration worker, was killed. King called for a four-day protest march to Montgomery. The marchers were assaulted by mobs of angry white

Martin Luther King, Jr., and his wife, Coretta Scott King, lead the historic Selma-to-Montgomery march in 1965. Media attention to the march sparked the public to pressure President Johnson to urge passage of the Voting Rights Act of 1965. Baez met the marchers in Montgomery.

racists with cattle prods and battered with clubs as millions of people watched on television.

King called for supporters to come from all over the country and join the rescheduled march. He warned them that it could be dangerous. Baez decided to go. On March 21, more than 5,000 people set off on the 4-day march as state troopers and members of the White Citizens Council rode in cars beside them, jeering and honking. There were 30,000 marchers by the time they reached Montgomery. Baez and dozens of other celebrities flew in for the last day. One demonstrator, Viola Liuzzo, was shot and killed as she drove down the airport road. Public pressure on President Johnson mounted until he went to Congress to urge the passage of the historic Voting Rights Act of 1965.

Returning to the tour, Baez found Dylan remote. Later she wrote, "I loved the fame, attention, and association with Bob, but soon our real differences surfaced." She was foolish to try to change things, he insisted.

Other friends were also angered by Dylan's turning his back on the civil rights movement. Phil Ochs, a protest singer and a friend of Dylan's from Folk City, was especially upset when Dylan wrote him that politics did not matter, that "the only thing that's real is inside you."

At the end of their tour, Dylan invited Baez to accompany him to England on a scheduled concert tour. She went along, booking her own London debut as well. She assumed that Dylan would bring her onstage as his guest.

At London's plush Savoy Hotel in May 1965, Dylan wore knee-length boots, silk shirts, and as usual, dark glasses. British fans loved him. To her surprise, Baez was not invited onstage with Dylan. She waited in the wings feeling wounded and powerless.

Baez performed at her own debut concert in London to a packed house. Her parents flew in from Paris, where Albert Baez was working for UNESCO. When the London tour was over, Dylan and Baez returned to the United States but parted company.

At the 1965 Newport Folk Festival, Dylan abandoned his folk guitar for an electric one. The move marked a drastic change in both Dylan's career and popular music in general. His new sound was more rock 'n' roll than folk. His new songs, cynical but brilliant dirges, had virtually no explicit political content. In the end, it seemed he was not as socially concerned as his folk contemporaries, more poetic than political.

Baez, on the other hand, returned from England to become even more involved in politics than she had been.

Baez and Dylan in London in 1965. That year the two began to drift apart: Dylan developed an interest in rock 'n' roll and began to perform with an electric guitar; Baez stuck with folk and criticized Dylan for not writing songs with social content. The two would not perform together again until 1975.

CHAPTER FIVE

Changing the World

By early 1965, the political folk music scene was being eclipsed by rock. Following the success of the Beatles, British bands were arriving in droves in hopes of making a splash stateside. The British invasion, as this musical wave of immigration is called, included such groups as the Searchers, the Hollies, the Kinks, the Yardbirds, and of course, the Who and the Rolling Stones. They attacked the charts with their electric guitars, drums, dynamic voices, and blues-based chord progressions. Before long, folk music was losing listeners to these British pop/rock combos. But then folk music was presented with a new social cause—the Vietnam War—and regained its footing in the world of popular music.

At first, few Americans even knew where Vietnam was. Then, in June 1971, when the *New York Times* published the *Pentagon Papers*, the truth emerged about U.S. policies there. One of the authors of the secret report, Daniel Ellsberg, was a former marine officer horrified by American war atrocities.

In 1965, the English group the Yardbirds topped both the U.S. and British charts with hits such as "Heart Full of Soul" and "For Your Love." At one time or another, rock guitar legends Jeff Beck, Eric Clapton, and Jimmy Page were members of the group, which was part of the so-called British invasion of American popular music during the mid-1960s.

As the *Pentagon Papers* revealed, the United States had opposed the Vietnamese people's struggle for independence for decades. Back in 1945, Ho Chi Minh, a popular independence fighter with communist ideals, had led a guerrilla army victory over both French and Japanese invaders, establishing the Democratic Republic of Vietnam. After British troops reestablished French rule in what became known as South Vietnam, the French fought Ho Chi Minh in a bloody eight-year war. Although amply aided by U.S. financing of their military supplies, the French lost. The 1954 Geneva Agreement guaranteed free elections within two years to reunify Vietnam. But the elections never occurred. Fearing a Ho Chi Minh landslide, the United States sent arms and military "advisers" to put in place their own puppet president, Ngo Dinh Diem.

Once again a guerrilla resistance movement, the National Liberation Front (NLF), started struggling for freedom, this time against "Yankee" aggressors. Under the Geneva Agreement, the Americans were allowed 685 military "advisers" in South Vietnam. The Kennedy administration secretly increased that figure to 16,000. Some took part in combat against the NLF. Diem was assassinated in 1963. The generals who took over were even less popular, and the NLF grew while U.S. involvement increased.

Baez was one of a handful of Americans who spoke out against the war from the start. She contributed $2,000 to help publicize the

In April of 1965, the Students for a Democratic Society (SDS) organized a demonstration at the White House to protest U.S. involvement in Vietnam. Some 25,000 people descended upon the nation's capital to participate in the demonstration. Baez contributed $2,000 to SDS and, along with folksingers Pete Seeger and Phil Ochs, provided music for the occasion.

first antiwar march on Washington, on April 17, 1965, organized by the Students for a Democratic Society (SDS). The march of 25,000 people marked a historic turning point in public opinion. There was now clearly strong opposition to U.S. foreign policy, which had been unopposed since the 1950s. Baez, Phil Ochs, Pete Seeger, and other folksingers performed for the demonstrators, who marched on the Capitol to petition Congress to bring an end to U.S. involvement in the war.

It was the largest peace march in U.S. history, yet television gave it only passing—and mostly negative—coverage. At the next demonstration in October, more than 100,000 people participated. As thousands of body bags carrying dead Americans began arriving from Vietnam, the news coverage improved.

Just days after that demonstration, 20,000 U.S. marines, using the pretext of "saving American lives," landed in the Dominican Republic to put down efforts to restore democracy, rubbed out by a military coup in 1963. The marines stopped the Dominicans in their tracks. More people began to doubt White House excuses. The press dubbed it Washington's "credibility gap."

On college campuses and in high schools, students demanded answers to their questions about Vietnam. Many schools conducted "teach-ins"—hours of debate and audience questions, sometimes televised. Soon, more people opposed the war.

Baez leapt into the fray. She could have made a lot of money by expanding her tour schedule and pushing her record sales even higher, but her social action voice cried out for release. To her parents she wrote, "I have a choice. . . . I want to start a peace movement. . . . The movement will be nonviolent. . . . I am a leader. . . . See you in jail!"

In the fall of 1965, Baez purchased an abandoned one-room schoolhouse near her home and, with Ira Sandperl, opened a school, the Institute for the Study of Nonviolence. Chosen on a first-come, first-served basis, students paid only $120 for a 6-week term, lodging and food included. Baez covered the extra costs out

Baez and Ira Sandperl, the director of the Institute for the Study of Nonviolence, at a press conference in 1967. The institute, which she cofounded, featured exercise to music, meditation, and discussion of books and ideas. At this press conference Baez announced that as a form of antiwar protest she would pay only 30 percent of her income tax, the portion that did not go to fund the U.S. military.

of her album royalties. Resentful of the rigidity of the schools she had attended, Baez created a much freer atmosphere at the institute. Four days a week, Baez and 15 students met for lunch, exercised to Beatles records, and then squatted on the bare floor to discuss books and ideas. On the fifth day everyone meditated.

The peaceful school soon had problems with neighbors. Dr. and Mrs. Gerald Petkuss, who lived across the road, filed a zoning violation complaint with the Monterey County Board of Supervisors. At the hearing, Baez sat calmly in the front row, wearing a businesslike dress and shoes on her usually bare feet. By a 3–2 vote, the institute was allowed to remain. To take the sting out of the controversial decision, the board formally requested area residents to fly American flags to show that "Kooks, Commies, and Cowards do not represent our country."

The institute lasted for almost a decade, later moving to Santa Cruz and changing its name to the Resource Center for Nonviolence.

In 1965, Baez met Martin Luther King, Jr., in South Carolina. She met him again in Grenada, Mississippi, the following year. She

In 1966, King and Baez lead a group of black children to enroll in an all-white public school in Grenada, Mississippi. The group was jeered and taunted by segregationists and racists along the way. Andrew Young (left), who later became a member of President Jimmy Carter's administration and then mayor of Atlanta, Georgia, is behind King.

was invited to be part of a group that would accompany black elementary school children as they entered a previously all-white public school for the first time. A line of name-calling adults stood threateningly on the sidelines while Baez and King, side by side, led the children into the school. Baez treasured forever a photograph of the scene.

Baez continued to give as many as 20 concerts a year, always mentioning the institute during the show and speaking out against the war in Vietnam. Gone was the remote Barefoot Madonna, the cool performer of 1959. Now she was a full-fledged activist, both onstage and off, and partly thanks to her the antiwar movement in the United States grew by leaps and bounds. In April 1967, a million people marched down New York's Fifth Avenue. A contingent of black demonstrators from Harlem linked up with the march, carrying handmade signs proclaiming No Vietnamese Ever Called Me Nigger! But Baez and Sandperl never formally allied themselves with the official antiwar movement. True, the gigantic protest marches were peaceful. But Baez and Sandperl felt that nonviolence was being applied as a temporary tactic, not as an overall philosophy. They feared that as the war intensified, frustration would breed violent behavior.

Baez's manager, Manny Greenhill, urged her to work harder on her career or risk losing it. In 1967, Baez agreed to a whirlwind two-month tour of Japan, Europe, and the United States.

In Japan, Baez was assigned an official translator named Takasaki. Still her audiences were not responsive to what she said to them about peace, war, and freedom. They also smiled at sad statements and looked sullen when she joked. In Hiroshima, where the United States had dropped the first atomic bomb to end World War II, Baez attended a peace rally where she discovered the truth about her translator. A friendly interpreter, Tsurumi, told her that Takasaki had deliberately mistranslated everything she said. The *New York Times* of February 21, 1967, told how "Harold Cooper, a CIA man, had ordered the Japanese interpreter . . . to substitute an innocuous translation in Japanese for Miss Baez's remarks in English on Vietnam."

In contrast, the European segment of the tour was joyful. Baez allowed herself to relax. She had an affair with a French photographer who took her dancing and shopping in Paris. She indulged in silk clothes and new shoes. In Austria, she rode horseback with a handsome count, and in Italy she shopped the famous Via Veneto with Furio Colombo, the acclaimed author and journalist. She stayed in a luxury hotel and had breakfast in bed. Later, Baez said she had "felt like the queen of the world."

Baez returned to tour the United States only to find that the Daughters of the American Revolution were refusing to allow her to sing in Philadelphia's Constitution Hall. After a public fuss, Baez received a permit for a free concert at the base of the Washington Monument. She returned home refreshed, ready for another cycle of political activity.

"See you in jail," Baez had written to her parents, and in October 1967 her prophecy came true. The week of October 16 was Stop the Draft Week. Activists who emphasized the right to self-defense intended to block the Oakland induction center for a few days. Baez and other pacifists planned a separate demonstration for Monday, October 16. Early in the morning, Baez joined two dozen others to sit at the entrance of the induction center. Several hundred people formed a picket line of support. As young inductees arrived by the busload, they were unable to enter the building. Baez and more than 100 other protesters were arrested. She and 35 other women were taken to Santa Rita Rehabilitation Center, where she served 10 days, most of it spent singing and talking to the other prisoners. Dr. King came to visit her, causing a stir.

The following day, 3,000 demonstrators came to the Oakland induction center, some wearing hard hats and garbage-can-lid shields. Helmeted police jumped them with clubs and mace, injuring scores. On Friday, 10,000 people gathered and set up barricades

Baez is caught in the fray as police break up an antiwar rally outside a naval base in Alameda, California. No longer just a performer at these protests, Baez was often among the organizers, and she would end up serving jail time for her part in the demonstrations.

in the streets near the induction center. More beatings and arrests followed.

Months later, Baez and her mother were jailed along with 60 other women during a similar action. Baez received a 45-day sentence. During her second stay in jail, Baez was told that David Harris, leader of the antidraft organization called the Resistance, was coming to visit her. Her life was about to change again.

Baez with husband David Victor Harris. Harris, an avowed antiwar activist, founded an organization called the Resistance, which urged young men to resist the draft in protest of U.S. military involvement in Vietnam.

CHAPTER SIX

Prisoner of Conscience

Wearing a bright dress instead of her drab prison garb, Baez waited anxiously in the cramped visitors' room. Then a six-foot-three, blue-eyed man with a cowboy hat perched on his head strode into the room. After their meeting, Baez was returned to her cell. When she and her mother were released, Baez contacted her supporters, met with the press, and called Harris.

David Victor Harris was born in Fresno, California, in 1946. At Stanford University, he was elected student body president in his junior year, 1966. A few months later, he returned his draft card to the Selective Service and dropped out of college. At an antiwar demonstration of 75,000 people in San Francisco on April 15, 1967, Harris announced the founding of a draft refusal organization called the Resistance.

Harris dropped out of college because he did not want to be included in the ranks of the privileged who used college as an easy way to get out of military service, leaving poorer youth, many of them from minority groups, to do the fighting and dying in Vietnam. Resisters such as Harris reported to their draft boards to refuse induction. They were put on trial—where they publicized their opposition to the war—and then were sentenced to long jail terms.

Completely immersed in Resistance work, Harris managed to find time for romance with Baez between speeches. They moved together into a Resistance commune near Stanford. Baez was nervous. She had shied away from serious love affairs since 1965. Baez often said, "The easiest kind of relationship for me is with 10,000 people. The hardest is with one."

In early January 1968, Harris refused induction into the military and was indicted by a grand jury. Awaiting trial, Harris went on tour with Baez and Sandperl. For the first time since Dylan's London tour, Baez was not the center of attention. Harris, about to go to jail for his principles, was the main attraction for audiences of draft-age men and their friends.

Only three months after they met, Baez and Harris were discussing marriage and children's names. Baez had fallen in love again, but this time the man she loved shared her political ideals and was "someone I don't just crave because his hair falls a certain way and his lips have a cupid's curl."

Their upcoming marriage was front-page news in the tabloids. *Time* magazine called it the "wedding of the century." The "Queen of Folk" was marrying, not the "King of Rock," but an antiwar martyr, a "draft dodger."

The day before the wedding, Baez became ill with a fever. Harris's Resistance friends, who had been flown in at Baez's expense, were having a bachelor party for Harris that night. Instead of attending the party, Harris took care of Baez.

They were married on March 26, 1968, in a church decorated with peace symbols. A pacifist minister performed a mixed Quaker-Episcopalian ceremony attended by family members, close friends, and "half the Resistance movement." A film crew photographed

A grim memorial to the Reverend Martin Luther King, Jr., who was murdered in April 1968. After King's assassination, blacks rose up in rebellion throughout cities in the South. U.S. National Guardsmen and federal troops were called in to quell the unrest.

Baez in a Grecian style, off-white, floor-length dress, her bare feet peeking out beneath it.

Just a few days later, on April 4, Martin Luther King, Jr., was assassinated by a hired gunman in Memphis, where King was supporting a strike of sanitation workers. In more than a hundred American cities, blacks rose up in rebellion, setting fire to poor neighborhoods. It took 65,000 National Guardsmen and federal troops to quell the uprising. Thirty-eight people were killed and more than 15,000 arrested. In the weeks prior to his death, King had made speeches connecting poverty and the Vietnam War. The FBI had tapped his telephones and sent him anonymous threatening letters. A Senate report on the FBI in 1976 stated that the FBI "tried to destroy Dr. King."

The press rushed to interview Baez on King's death. She discussed her political differences with the civil rights leader. He had wanted to win a share of the American dream for black people. Baez believed that the election of corrupt black officials would change nothing. It took Baez years to realize what King's ideas had meant in her life. By then, there were many elected black politicians. But the lives of most black Americans had grown worse, and now Martin Luther King was dead.

Baez's worst fears of violence in the antiwar movement materialized in the summer of 1968. By then the movement had spread to Europe and Japan, and President Johnson had announced that he would not seek the Democratic party nomination, so tarnished was his name by the horrors of the Vietnam War. The 1968 Democratic convention in Chicago turned into a violent brawl when it became clear to thousands of antiwar activists that the peace candidate, George McGovern, would not win the nomination. Running against Richard Nixon in the fall would be Vice-president Hubert Humphrey, who shared Johnson's position on the war.

Chicago mayor Richard Daley decided to use force against peace advocates, both inside the convention hall and on the city streets. A thousand police with riot guns, clubs, and tear gas rampaged through the city, attacking people who looked as though they might be antiwar demonstrators. By the end of the week, 1 man was dead, 1,000 had been injured, and more than 660 had been arrested. Thousands of people joined the antiwar movement following the violence in Chicago.

Meanwhile, Harris and Baez concentrated their energies on the Resistance, by then almost completely isolated from the rest of the mass protest movement. Baez's life changed totally. She had looked forward to being a wife and mother, but the reality was considerably different from the fantasy. She lived with her husband on a small plot of land they named Struggle Mountain, where the privacy Baez had always treasured was nonexistent. Their ramshackle house was attached to another twin shack, and a large communal house was nearby.

Harris was popular with young men facing the draft, but the young women of the budding feminist movement did not care much for him. For one thing, he called women "chicks." Then the Resistance put out an antidraft poster showing Baez and her two sisters, all dressed up, with the caption Girls Say Yes to Boys Who Say No. It went on sale to raise funds for the Resistance. As Baez told the story later, three "women's libbers" came to complain about the poster, upset by the idea, even if expressed with humor, that women would offer their bodies as a reward to men who opposed the draft. Baez and Harris saw nothing wrong with the poster, but feminists were furious with both of them.

At his trial, Harris was found guilty as expected. In April 1969, on a speaking tour with Harris as he awaited sentencing, Baez learned that she was pregnant. Three months later, on July 15, the sheriff showed up, handcuffed Harris, and carted him off to a federal prison in Arizona.

All through 1968 and 1969, the antiwar movement grew. By the end of 1969, 34,000 men had refused induction. Each month in Oakland nearly half the men called by the draft board never appeared. In Vietnam, desertions skyrocketed. Working-class "grunts" began "fragging" the quarters of their ROTC college graduate officers (tossing grenades into them). Returning veterans formed a group called Vietnam Veterans Against the War (VVAW). VVAW members, some in wheelchairs, led antiwar marches.

In early 1969, a guilt-ridden Vietnam vet revealed that on March 16, 1968, a company of soldiers went to the Vietnamese village of My Lai, rounded up 450 people, mostly aged men and women and young children, ordered them into a ditch, and mowed them down with machine-gun fire. Other soldiers noted that such slaughters added to the "body count" reported by officers to television reporters to make it look as though America was winning the war. Under tremendous public pressure, several officers were put on trial for the My Lai massacre, but only one, Lieutenant William Calley, was found guilty. He was sentenced to life imprisonment and released after three years, most of which he spent under house arrest at home. By contrast, David Harris spent nearly two years in harsh federal prisons for refusing to go to Vietnam.

The antiwar movement continued to gain momentum. By late 1970, when a Gallup poll asked Americans whether or not "the United States should withdraw all troops from Vietnam by the end of next year," 65 percent of those polled said that it should.

In 1969, a summer music festival took place outside Woodstock, New York, an outpost for New York City artists, musicians, and writers since the very early part of the 20th century. During the 1960s, Dylan had a house there, as did Irish singer Van Morrison and hipster Frank Zappa, the leader of the avant-garde rock/jazz group the Mothers of Invention. Poets Gregory Corso and Allen Ginsberg, the latter a favorite of Dylan's, visited Woodstock frequently. The music festival, which was actually held in Bethel but took the name of the nearby artistic mecca, was a major moment in the history of popular music and marked the end of one of the most tumultuous periods in American history—the 1960s.

Woodstock was more than just a music festival. It was about peace, love, and compassion for all people; it was a cry for freedom, racial harmony, and honest government in America; and it was a call for an end to the war in Vietnam. A half million people came to Woodstock to hear some of the finest musical talent of the day. Still, few could have known that they were about to take part in a historic event.

Entrances to the New York State Thruway had to be closed because of the overwhelming volume of traffic, which moved at a snail's pace all the way to the Woodstock exit. By their sheer number, the enormous crowd forced the promoters to declare the concert, which began as a paid event, free to the public when it became clear that it would be impossible to sell tickets to everyone who wanted them or to turn away so many people. Baez, six months pregnant and with her mother beside her, was scheduled to perform at the festival and had to take a helicopter to get there.

It rained almost constantly on the festival crowd for three days, and everyone was soaked and muddy. People shared food, cooking supplies, blankets. They bathed and washed their jeans and tie-dyed shirts and dresses in nearby ponds. Some had tents, but most slept under the stars. Their ears were treated to the sounds of countless top-name performers, including Crosby, Stills, Nash and Young; Sly and the Family Stone; the Who; the Grateful Dead; and the legendary rock guitarist Jimi Hendrix. Solo singers such as Arlo Guthrie, John Sebastian, Phil Ochs, and Janis Joplin also performed. There were a few arrests for drug possession, and some were arrested for skinny-dipping, but generally there was no

Graham Nash (left) and David Crosby of the folk rock group Crosby, Stills, Nash and Young perform at the Woodstock festival in August 1969. A half million people traveled to the Upstate New York town of Bethel to attend the three-day concert and hear folk and rock superstars such as the Who, Jimi Hendrix, Janis Joplin, and Joan Baez.

trouble with the law. In fact, many were surprised at how peaceful the enormous gathering was. The music and the rain seemed to go on forever.

Baez, staying in a nearby hotel, came onstage in the middle of the night to sing to the residents of what she would always think of as the "golden city." She sang "Joe Hill" and a moving rendition of the spiritual "Swing Low Sweet Chariot." The feeling of togetherness wrought in the struggles of the 1960s created an atmosphere of cooperation at Woodstock that made Baez write years later, "There can never be another Woodstock." Just weeks later, most of the "Woodstock nation," as those who were at the festival came to be called, participated in a work moratorium. Millions of Americans broke up their usual routines in order to attend teach-ins and debate the Vietnam War at their workplaces. There was a belief and a hope that the spirit of the Woodstock music festival could be carried over into the 1970s and beyond.

Following her appearance at Woodstock, Baez recorded an entire double record album of Dylan songs and another album she dedicated to David Harris. She wrote to Harris every day, decorating her letters with drawings of herself with a swollen belly performing Lamaze exercises. Despite the weight she had gained, she trekked back and forth for frequent visits with her husband in depressing prison visiting rooms.

Baez returned to Struggle Mountain to have her baby, wishing that Harris could be with her for the important event. Instead, a friend, Gail Zermeno, accompanied her during her natural childbirth classes and the actual birth. When they handed Baez her newborn son, Gabriel Harris, she sang a Joe Cocker song to him entitled "Hello Little Friend." As soon as her strength was back, Baez went traveling again, taking the baby with her to Poland, Italy, and Switzerland.

After organizing a strike to protest prison conditions, Harris was transferred to La Tuna Correctional Facility in Texas, 1,500 miles away. The incarcerated men called the prison Siberia, and from Baez's point of view, it was far enough away to be called that. Still, she flew in every month.

The long separation from Harris was taking its toll. Later, Baez revealed that she "felt that his being a prisoner was making me a prisoner." Baez had to keep up "the image society had of us together." But at times "I wanted to abandon all responsibility to everyone in the world and to run, to flee, to be wild. . . . And occasionally I did all these things."

In her 1987 autobiography, Baez revealed that after Harris was in jail for 10 months she had an affair. "I sneaked around, got hot flashes when the phone rang, made mysterious trips to Los Angeles, and worried about being a terrible person. I was frightened of David's homecoming."

Then, on March 15, 1971, Harris was paroled. Baez went with Gabriel to bring him home, photographers accompanying them. There were press conferences at the airport and a party at the Institute for Nonviolence. It was several hours before they were finally alone. Baez told her husband all of the things that had gone on in her life for the past 20 months, including her affair.

Readjustment proved impossible. Baez tired of hearing Harris tell his stories of prison violence over and over to "adoring groupies." She also had great difficulty sharing Gabriel after so many months alone with him. They were divorced in 1973, never airing their grievances in public. Baez insisted later that her affair was not the cause of the breakup. "I couldn't breathe, and I couldn't try anymore to be a wife. . . . I belonged alone." In her autobiography she wrote, "I am made to live alone. I cannot possibly live in the same house with anyone." After the divorce, Baez went to live in Woodside, California, Harris stayed in the hills half an hour away, and son Gabriel visited back and forth.

"I am sorry, Gabe," Baez wrote to Gabriel in 1987, "that we couldn't be a family. I think I have been a good mother. I have loved you very much." And she added to Harris, "We did our absolute best. We are still doing it."

Antiwar protesters demonstrate outside the Capitol in Washington, D.C., in 1971. The return of many veterans from the Vietnam War who recalled atrocities they witnessed there combined with the publication of the Pentagon Papers to raise sentiment against the war to a fevered pitch during the early 1970s.

CHAPTER SEVEN

End of an Era

The beginning of the end of the Vietnam War came in the spring of 1970 when President Nixon, the 1968 "peace candidate," ordered the invasion of Vietnam's neighbor, Cambodia. Campuses erupted in protest. On May 4, at Ohio's Kent State University, a National Guard unit fired on student demonstrators, killing four and paralyzing one. When the news spread, students and professors at more than 400 colleges and universities called the first general student strike in U.S. history.

Antiwar protests swept the country like a storm. Prowar senators known as hawks switched sides and joined the so-called peace-seeking doves. On May 14, at Jackson State College, an all-black school in Mississippi, city police and state highway patrol officers sprayed bullets on student protesters gathered near a women's dormitory. Two fell dead; 14 were wounded. Instantly, black colleges across the country joined the strike.

The usual June commencements that year turned into peace demonstrations. At the University of Massachusetts, 2,600 grad-

uates marched to the beat of a funeral drum, wearing peace symbols and doves on their graduation gowns, fists raised in protest.
In December, hundreds of VVAW members in Detroit testified with
tears streaming down their faces to atrocities they had witnessed or
committed against Vietnamese civilians. In April 1971, more than
1,000 veterans threw their medals over the White House fence.

More protest marches forced Nixon to fulfill his pledge to withdraw U.S. troops, but he did so with a new Vietnamization strategy. America would leave Vietnam, but there would be little left for the victors except a bombed-out wasteland. U.S. bombers dropped tons of explosives on North Vietnam—more tonnage than all the bombs dropped over Europe and Japan during World War II. Still, as American soldiers came home, many Americans believed that the war was ending.

Baez knew better. She could not forget the bombs raining down on the children of Vietnam. When Ira Sandperl came up with an idea for keeping the war in the public eye, Baez started organizing

A soldier looks over the bodies that litter the streets of Phnom Penh, Cambodia's capital, in 1975. The bombing of Cambodia was a desperate effort by Richard Nixon to thwart the communist presence in Southeast Asia.

Ring Around the Congress, a plan for women and children to encircle Congress, joining hands in symbolic solidarity with the women and children of Vietnam, to demand an end to U.S. violence.

Martin Luther King's widow, Coretta King, took to the idea immediately and met with Baez in New York. Prominent women's organizations sent out hundreds of thousands of letters announcing the action. Baez happily envisioned as many as 100,000 women and children joining hands around Congress on June 22. Instead, the project became what Baez later called "the most difficult, demoralizing, battering, discouraging task I have ever taken on in my life."

First, Coretta King suddenly withdrew from the leadership. Then, when Sandperl and Baez flew to Washington, D.C., to set up a national headquarters for the action, they encountered major trouble from Marion Barry, then chairman of the D.C. school board. Intent on painting the antiwar movement as racist, Barry led a campaign to discredit the protest. Eventually, he succeeded in smearing the demonstration.

Other black community leaders asserted that Barry and his handful of supporters did not speak for the black community, but it was too late, the damage had been done. The turnout was poor. Women had to stretch their arms wide to form their ring around the White House.

A less committed person might have dropped out of sight after such an ordeal, but not Baez. A Vietnamese group, the Committee for Solidarity with the American People, invited her and three other Americans to visit North Vietnam and witness the destruction in order to encourage Americans to step up their flagging efforts to stop the killing. Her travel companions would be a conservative lawyer, a liberal Episcopalian minister, and an outspoken Vietnam veteran. It seemed like a safe enough journey. With peace negotiations resumed and a cease-fire in place for the upcoming Christmas season, the bombing and fighting had almost stopped. They would

From left to right: Mike Allen, Baez, and Barry Romo walk through the rubble of Gialam International Airport in Hanoi. During their visit they were met by a barrage of American B-52s that bombed the North Vietnamese capital continuously for 10 days in December 1973.

tour North Vietnam and deliver holiday mail to American prisoners of war in Hanoi. Baez arranged to leave Gabriel with his father and be back to him by Christmas Day.

For two days, the delegation was wined and dined by their North Vietnamese hosts. Baez sang peace songs, and they visited war memorials and music schools where, to her surprise, many of the children knew her songs. She had no way of knowing that President Nixon was making what he later called his "most difficult decision," an unrelenting Christmas bombing of Hanoi.

When Baez and the others were shown disturbing films about the effects of poison chemicals and napalm used by U.S. soldiers in

Vietnam, she got up to leave the room, unable to bear the horrors. Suddenly, the room went dark and sirens wailed. Nixon's Christmas presents had arrived. They all rushed to an underground shelter and listened to bombs exploding above them. There were 10 more raids that same night.

For 11 nights the B-52 bombing continued. Each morning Baez emerged to check the damage. Bach Mai Hospital was largely destroyed, despite the Red Cross symbol on its roof. At the edge of a bomb crater, Baez heard a mother singing a strange, beautiful song. She asked her interpreter to translate the words. His answer became the title of her new album when she returned home, *Where Are You Now, My Son?*—with the sounds of bombs, sirens, and weeping mothers in the background.

When B-52s were shot down, surviving crews were taken prisoner. Baez went to visit the American prisoners. They were bandaged and pale with shock. One captured pilot told her that he did not understand what was happening. Had not Secretary of State Henry Kissinger said that peace was at hand?

"Maybe he didn't mean it. They lie a lot," Baez responded. She sang "Kumbaya" for them, "No more bombing lord, Kumbaya" and hugged them. "Get us out of here . . . if you can," one pleaded as she left.

The delegation was having its own problems leaving Vietnam. The airport had been bombed and there was no way to fly home for Christmas. During a makeshift Christmas celebration, sirens sounded and once again they raced for the shelter. The Chinese embassy finally managed to arrange their departure.

Baez reached California on New Year's Day, 1973, and spent two weeks at Harris's house with Gabriel, recovering and giving interviews about her visit to North Vietnam. For a long time, the sound of a plane flying overhead terrified her.

Before the trip to Vietnam, Ginetta Sagan from the human rights group Amnesty International had visited Baez, bringing testimony and horrifying photographs of tortured political prisoners. Sagan had been a member of the antifascist underground in Italy during World War II and had herself been imprisoned and tortured. Amnesty worked for the release of "prisoners of conscience"—those arrested because of their religious or political beliefs—and to put an end to torture and to abolish the death penalty. Baez agreed to help organize an Amnesty chapter on the West Coast, hoping to reach the inaccessible people frightened by her tax refusals, draft resistance, and jail terms. She spent a year organizing Amnesty chapters and became a member of Amnesty's national advisory board.

Even as the Vietnam War drew to a close, Baez had little time for rest. Nightly newscasts were filled with footage of marches and rallies by other social groups that had learned how to organize from the civil rights and antiwar movements. Native Americans, farm workers, prisoners, Chicanos, Puerto Ricans, and gays all struggled for their own particular demands. Most of them asked Baez, one of the few performers still active in social struggles, to lend a hand.

She did. Somehow she managed to juggle her time between her young son and rallies, concerts, and recording dates. Whereas many others said they were "burned out" from the 1960s, Baez seemed as fired up as ever.

Still considered a folksinger by most people, Baez expanded her repertoire in an effort to prove her musical versatility. She recorded another album of Dylan songs, some country music, her own compositions, an album in Spanish, and even a poetry reading. She switched from the Vanguard label to A & M, a larger company more financially able to take risks. One of her last Vanguard releases, a remake of Robbie Robertson's "The Night They Drove Old Dixie Down," remained on the top-40 list for 15 weeks.

Most often, Baez combined her singing career with her Amnesty activism. One of Amnesty's major areas of concern was Latin America, where barbaric military dictatorships were in power. In jails overflowing with dissidents, torturers plied their grisly trade, sometimes using sophisticated techniques taught to them by U.S. advisers.

Chile was a short-lived exception that would deeply affect the lives of folksingers all over the world, including Baez and Phil Ochs. In the fall of 1970, a democratic socialist, Salvador Allende, was elected president of Chile. When the news of his election reached the White House, Nixon and Kissinger immediately took action to topple the freely elected Chilean government. "Squeeze Chile's economy until it screams," Nixon ordered. All U.S. aid was cut off—except military aid. On September 11, 1973, the Chilean air force bombed the presidential palace, and General Augusto Pinochet's troops forced their way in. Within a few hours, Allende lay dead.

What followed was a nightmare. Thousands of soldiers swept through the streets killing or arresting those suspected of being Allende supporters. A few managed to flee or hide in embassy buildings. More than 10,000 were taken to the national soccer stadium, where many were tortured and killed. One of the victims was Victor Jara, the most famous figure in the New Chilean Song Movement. As Jara started playing his music to lift the spirits of the stadium's detainees, Pinochet's goons rushed him, broke his fingers, smashed his guitar, and beat him to death.

Baez and Ochs were stunned. Ochs had already become saddened by the decline in antiwar activity and had visited Chile during the Allende presidency and grown close to Jara. Now a traumatized Ochs tried to organize a New York benefit concert for Chilean refugees. Ticket sales went nowhere until Ochs corralled Bob Dylan and told him the story of Chile in music and words. Dylan agreed to perform at the benefit, and the house was full.

Baez devoted herself full-time to Amnesty International, raising money at benefit concerts to assist Pinochet's victims and publicize his crimes. In 1974, she toured Venezuela, where many Chilean refugees had fled after the coup, and met Orlando Latelier, ambassador and foreign minister to the United States during Allende's presidency. He had been imprisoned during the Pinochet coup but was freed after an international campaign on his behalf. When he left the prison camp, Latelier was warned by the authorities to watch his step.

Latelier refused to remain silent. He moved near Washington, D.C., and worked to rally opposition to Chile's dictatorship. Soon, he would pay dearly for his courage—and Baez would be the feature singer at a very sad event.

Meanwhile, in 1975 the Vietnam War—the longest in American history—finally ended. North Vietnamese and NLF forces swept through South Vietnam to unify their country. Baez and Ochs sang a duet at The War Is Over free concert that Ochs organized in Central Park on Mother's Day, 1975. Many from the Newport and Folk City crowd appeared—Seeger and Odetta among others. It was a fitting final chorus to the 1960s protest music era, but Baez's two voices were far from stilled.

Baez and Dylan give a benefit performance together at Clinton State Prison in 1975 for former boxer Rubin "Hurricane" Carter. The performance was part of Dylan's Rolling Thunder Revue tour, which featured artists such as Joni Mitchell, Arlo Guthrie, Roberta Flack, and the poet Allen Ginsberg.

CHAPTER EIGHT

Three Voices Together

Despite her experience with him in London in 1965, Baez joined Bob Dylan and his Rolling Thunder Revue tour in 1975. According to her sister Mimi, she "hung in there all those years out of some kind of really wild feeling for him."

Dylan, who had secretly married Sara Lowndes in 1965, had gone on to have four children with her. He earned $80,000 a month from his tours. In 1973, Dylan and Sara had built a $2-million domed mansion in Malibu, California. By then, rock 'n' roll had split into several different categories, and no one was sure whether Dylan's music would fit in. New stars were on the music scene—Pink Floyd, Led Zeppelin, Cat Stevens, Elton John.

While Dylan's concerts sold out and his albums shot up the charts, his marriage broke up. He returned to Greenwich Village, leaving his family behind in California.

By 1975, Greenwich Village had changed. Most of the coffeehouses had become tourist traps or were replaced by falafel stands, Greek restaurants, or overpriced Indian clothing stores.

Dylan holed up in his house during the day writing songs, emerging at night to roam the few remaining clubs.

It was around that time that he conceived of a tour that would never stop—sort of a circuslike road show, with one band and many performers, traveling together forever—The Rolling Thunder Revue. Dylan and some friends began listing potential performers. Ochs was considered, but everyone thought he would be a problem. Since Chile, Ochs had been drinking nonstop. Baez's name was mentioned, but no one believed she would agree to come after her souring experience of 10 years earlier. Dylan picked up the phone and arranged to meet her in New York City later in the summer. Baez eventually signed to spend a year on the road.

Baez was one of 70 people aboard 3 chartered buses that left New York on October 27, 1975. The poet Allen Ginsberg, singers Joni Mitchell and Arlo Guthrie, even a gypsy violinist were among those making the trip. Like one big happy family, Sara Dylan, trying for a reconciliation, came along with her mother and the children. Baez brought her own mother, her sister Mimi, and her son, Gabe, and a friend of his. Dylan's mother even came for part of the tour, and in Toronto, Dylan, who had kept his Jewish parents a secret for so many years, brought her onstage.

Baez saved the day at one near-fiasco performance at a prison in Clinton, New Jersey. The audience cheered when Dylan introduced his song about a prisoner, former boxing champion Rubin "Hurricane" Carter, who was trying to clear himself of a 1966 murder conviction. But Dylan's other songs and those of most of the singers drew hoots and catcalls. Everyone expected Joan Baez to be treated with even greater rudeness, but when she sang a rhythmic version of "Land of 1000 Dances," dancing all over the stage and then bringing an inmate up to do the limbo with her, she was an instant success.

Off and on during the tour, Dylan and Baez were involved in the filming of *Renaldo and Clara*, a hodgepodge of plotless episodes. Women in the Rolling Thunder Revue, including Baez, all played prostitutes. When the film was released two years later, one critic said that it "sank so many reputations, it's like watching the defeat of the Spanish Armada." Still, Baez and Dylan enjoyed clowning together while making the film. For instance, Baez dressed up as a Dylan look-alike, and they sang together.

The first half of the Rolling Thunder tour ended in Madison Square Garden on December 8, 1975. Later, Baez commented that the tour had been like "an incredibly happy family."

The second half of the tour was starkly unhappy by contrast. Dylan stayed on the road between Rolling Thunder segments, but things did not go well. Too many drugs were around, and a Houston, Texas, crowd, still remembering Dylan's civil rights days, did not exactly welcome him. He was relieved when the time came to join the original tour group in Florida. But tragic news about Phil Ochs quickly cast a pall over the entire group.

Not invited to accompany Rolling Thunder, Ochs had increased his drinking. Some nights he slept on the street, and he grew hostile, even violent. At his sister's home on April 9, 1976, Ochs hanged himself. When Dylan heard about Ochs's death, he took the news very badly. Things turned sour, and the tour broke up.

On September 21, 1976, Baez learned of the death of her Chilean friend Orlando Latelier. A bomb placed under Latelier's car by Michael Townley, an American agent of the Pinochet regime, had exploded, killing Latelier and Ronni Moffitt, a young woman who worked with him. Friends pressed for justice, and Townley was extradited; he told the truth in exchange for a brief sentence.

Baez flew to Washington and sang to a weeping audience at a memorial service. Back home she was plagued by nightmares about Latelier. She had started to write her autobiography but she set the project aside. Latelier's death had shocked her. She decided to give more time to social causes.

But Baez recognized that for her international humanitarian work to succeed she would have to maintain her reputation as a singer. In the mid-1970s, that was a difficult thing to do. Folk music was commercially passé, and Baez was still known as a folksinger. Worse yet, Baez realized that the high notes of her "pure soprano" were disappearing.

She recorded her first nonpolitical album—*Diamonds and Rust*—and *From Every Stage*, a double album. She then toured to promote her albums, something she had never had to do in the past. Soon *Diamonds and Rust* went gold.

Baez switched from A & M to a label called Portrait, on the verge of becoming a CBS subsidiary. The jacket cover of her first album with Portrait, *Blowin' Away*, showed Baez wearing flight goggles and a silver racing-car jacket with an American flag sewn on its sleeve. Baez commented later that the cover "reflected my state of total confusion about my music and the direction of my life." She recorded another album, *Honest Lullaby*, publicizing it in the face of a tidal wave of heavy metal music. Both her albums were only modestly successful.

It was hard for Baez to realize that she was no longer a "hot item." She had done what she could to keep her career intact. She could not or would not become a heavy metal or punk star; nor could she change the whims of musical taste. She had pushed her albums, improved her voice, and updated her music. Now, close to the end of the 1970s and nearing her 40th birthday, Baez's social conscience was ready to take to the road again. This time, many former friends would become enemies.

Most people who had fought against U.S. policy in Vietnam felt it was ill advised to criticize the new unified government of that ruined nation. Not Baez. She told an interviewer in 1980 that she was "not political. I believe in people not systems. I don't have any ideological yoke around my neck that blinds me to human rights violations." She only knew that in Southeast Asia, thousands of people were suffering.

In 1979, with her old friend from Amnesty, Ginetta Sagan, Baez formed a study group on international affairs. Baez became aware

Baez and Ginetta Sagan of Amnesty International speak at a 1979 press conference in Los Angeles about human rights violations in Vietnam. Though the United States was no longer involved in Southeast Asia, Baez maintained an interest in the region, signing and sending with 81 others a letter to the Vietnamese government in an effort to help Vietnamese political prisoners, who were often beaten and tortured by their captors.

of the horrifying situation continuing in all of Southeast Asia from two visitors, a former student from Saigon and a Buddhist monk. The student had been persecuted by the Vietnamese "liberators" and the monk had been defrocked. Vietnam was in a shambles. U.S. crimes there had caused the victors to strike out blindly at anyone suspected of having ties to the Americans. Thousands of political prisoners were languishing in jails called reeducation camps. The promised reparation money from the United States had never arrived, so the Vietnamese government had broken its promises of no reprisals. The two refugees asked Baez why people who had struggled to end the Vietnam War were not speaking out against the human rights violations.

What followed was Baez's "Open Letter to the Socialist Republic of Vietnam," appealing to the Hanoi government for the improvement of human rights conditions. Eighty-one prominent people signed the Open Letter, and $53,000 was raised to publish it in 4 major dailies. Some former peace movement activists, including Jane Fonda, urged Baez to reconsider publishing the Open Letter. Others attacked her ferociously. A campaign was launched to stop Baez. Baez and Sagan met with the UN observer-ambassador from Vietnam and offered not to publish the letter if Amnesty International representatives were allowed to visit Vietnam within six months with free access to go where they chose. The ambassador refused, insisting that there were no human rights violations in Vietnam—and the letter was published.

Brickbats were hurled at Baez. She was "a CIA rat" engaging in a "cruel and wanton act" of betrayal of the Vietnamese. A counterstatement entitled "The Truth About Vietnam" was signed by 56 prominent people and appeared in the *New York Times*. It said that the people of Vietnam received free "education, medicine, and health care—human rights we in the United States have yet to achieve."

For a while, Baez was the darling of some political right-wingers who had supported the war. Ronald Reagan, then governor of California, gushed over her action on his weekly radio show. When Baez later toured Latin America and publicized the human rights violations of the United States under President Reagan, he remained silent.

Baez felt satisfied when she learned that the Vietnamese government, embarrassed by all the publicity, released some prisoners. After the Open Letter incident, she set up her own human rights organization, Humanitas. Smaller than Amnesty and without an elaborate apparatus, Humanitas could move more quickly in emergencies. Under its auspices, Baez took up her next cause—the plight of about 15 million refugees on the Cambodian border.

When U.S.-led South Vietnamese troops had invaded Cambodia in 1970, provoking the largest demonstrations ever in the United States, the Khmer Rouge guerrillas led by Pol Pot had

A mushroom cloud provides a stark contrast to the beautiful foliage after an American air attack near O Dar, Cambodia. Americans were outraged to learn that while the United States was pulling out of Vietnam, the bombing of communist forces in Cambodia continued.

driven the Vietnamese back. By then, Nixon's B-52 bombers had reduced Cambodia's cities to rubble. People were dying from famine and pestilence, and the Khmer Rouge government had ordered them into the countryside, where they could at least grow food. Those who resisted the policy—some 2 million—were slaughtered. Cambodia's "killing fields" shocked the world.

The "new revolutionary" Vietnamese government had feasted its eye on Cambodia for a long time, and the terrorism of Pol Pot gave it an opening. It invaded Cambodia, defeated the Pol Pot forces, and set up an occupation government. In 1979, Vietnam also sent its armies into neighboring Laos, where U.S. "advisers" had earlier engaged in a secret war against the Pathet Lao guerrilla force, using Mung tribesmen as cannon fodder. From both war-torn areas, thousands of terrified people fled the endless bloodshed, streaming into the area's only peaceful country, Thailand. They took flimsy boats into the South China Sea, braving storms and high waves to escape. Camps along the border were set up to hold suffering families.

Baez wondered why the Sixth Fleet of the U.S. Navy could not rescue the "boat people," and Sagan suggested a fund-raiser concert for them near the White House. Perhaps U.S. president Jimmy Carter, who had spoken out for human rights during his 1976 election campaign, would be open to the suggestion.

On July 19, 1979, after informing President Carter that the planned concert at the Lincoln Memorial was not a protest but a plea for help for the boat people, Baez performed for 10,000 people and then led a candlelight march to the White House. Back in her hotel room she turned on the television to see President Carter come out on the White House lawn and announce that the Sixth Fleet would be sent on a rescue mission.

After another fund-raiser in October, Baez flew to Thailand with a film crew and took an overnight train and a van from Bangkok to a refugee camp on the northern border. On the bank of the river, she saved a group of Laotians who had swum across to

Baez at a Thailand refugee camp in 1979. Her performance in Thailand, broadcast to millions on American television, raised more than $1 million for her human rights group Humanitas.

Thailand and were trying to climb ashore to safety while a Thai border patrol threatened to shoot them. Baez embarrassed the colonel in charge by kneeling at his feet and begging him to spare the lives of the refugees. She promised to dedicate a song to him at her evening concert if she heard that the people in the water were safely ashore. Whether the danger of unfavorable publicity or Baez's appeal did the trick, the swimmers came ashore safely.

That evening, thousands of refugees heard Baez sing. In the United States, television viewers had their first look at the hungry and ragged people of Southeast Asia, making it possible for Humanitas to raise more than $1 million to assist the suffering people who had come to hear the world-renowned human rights fighter and singer serenade them.

On July 13, 1985, under a hot sun, Baez stepped before a battery of microphones and spoke these words: "Good morning, children of the eighties! This is your Woodstock!" Then she launched into a rousing rendition of "Amazing Grace."

It was the precedent-setting Live Aid concert, held simultaneously in Philadelphia and London. Aimed at raising money to feed the world's hungry, Live Aid was televised around the world via satellite. One writer called it "the most spectacular global pop show and fund raising event in history." A reporter informed Baez that only four of the dozens of performers who had appeared in Woodstock in 1969 had been asked to sing for Live Aid—herself, the Who, Santana, and Crosby, Stills, and Nash.

By the early 1990s, when television viewers watched Baez in concert, she was still touring the world and making records after more than 30 years. An astute observer would have noticed that Baez's three interests—music, social activism, and plain everyday fun—seemed in perfect harmony.

From the middle of the 1970s into the 1990s, Baez's tour schedule was heavy, but she usually combined it with appearances for human rights causes. In 1976, she went to embattled Northern Ireland and marched with the peace movement there.

She refused to appear in Spain when the dictator Francisco Franco ran the country like a gigantic prison camp. One year after his death, in 1977, Baez came and sang songs and told stories informing young Spaniards about the history of their own civil war in the 1930s.

In 1978, in Ulm, Germany, she was sandwiched in as an experiment between Frank Zappa and the progressive rock band Genesis. The press reported that Baez "stole the show."

In the summer of that same year, Baez was scheduled to sing in the Soviet Union with Santana and the Beach Boys. When the Soviet regime canceled the concert, she journeyed to the city of

Gorki, where Nobel Peace Prize winner Andrei Sakharov and his wife, Elena Bonner, were living in forced exile. This was before Soviet leader Mikhail Gorbachev's free speech era of *glasnost* (openness), and Sakharov had earned the wrath of the authorities for his dissident ideas. When Sakharov and Bonner were first sent into exile, Baez had called them on the telephone and sung "We Shall Overcome" to them—a song known internationally, despite language differences. Now she went to their home with a reporter and a Russian-speaking photographer, knowing that publicity would help them gain their freedom again.

Throughout the 1980s, Baez set up groups of European supporters of Humanitas, taking time in between her songs to persuade her audiences to help the cause. In the United States, entrenched in the conservative policies of Ronald Reagan and

Cesar Chavez, second from left, the embattled leader of the United Farm Workers union, walks a picket line in Delano, California, in 1965. The union sought to improve the plight of migrant farm workers, who were mainly Mexicans and Mexican Americans. Baez sympathized with their cause and performed at a benefit for the union.

George Bush, only a few performers sang songs about social problems. Jackson Browne was one. Baez sang with him at a benefit for Cesar Chavez's United Farm Workers, an organization that was helping migrant workers, mostly Mexicans, like her father.

Baez did best in Europe where the youth were more conscious of the world around them. But she did not give up on American youth. Wherever she appeared, she told stories about injustices in the United States and other countries and urged young people to participate in struggles—to wake up and be part of the world.

On March 24, 1980, Baez sang at a memorial service in Washington, D.C., commemorating the death of El Salvador's Archbishop Oscar Romero, assassinated by one of the death squads of the undemocratic government long supported by the United States. The archbishop's murder inspired Baez to concentrate on Latin America for a year. In Argentina, she was teargassed and tossed out of her hotel. Bomb threats at her press conference turned up two very real bombs. In Chile, her concerts were banned by the Pinochet dictatorship, but 7,000 young people attended one anyway, the hall surrounded by police. In Brazil, where she also was banned from singing, Baez stood outside a government building and loudly sang "Gracias a la Vida" until a Brazilian congressman took her to a meeting place where she sang.

On the way home, Baez stopped in Nicaragua, where the dictator Anastasio Somoza had been toppled in 1979 by the Sandinistas, a youthful guerrilla group. Tomás Borge, minister of the Interior, took her on a tour of a prison packed with former members of the national guard, the U.S.-trained police force that had run roughshod over the country during the 45-year Somoza dynasty. Baez's presence motivated Borge to free a few very young prisoners. One of them, a boy of 16, had languished in prison for 3 years after he had been arrested with his national guard father. Baez was also shown the cell where Borge had been kept for years by Somoza's goons with his wrists chained together and his head covered with a sack.

Baez did not believe that the cruelty of Somoza justified prisoners in the new revolutionary Nicaragua. But she bemoaned the policies of her government that forced the impoverished Nicaraguans to invest in a self-defense army against the vicious attacks of U.S.-directed "contras" (former national guard members). From footage of Baez's tour, PBS produced a film, *There But for Fortune—Joan Baez in Latin America*, bringing before the public the sorry information about U.S. policy in neighboring countries.

In 1982, Baez performed for Peace Week, an appeal for a nuclear freeze. On June 6—Peace Sunday—at the Rose Bowl in Pasadena, California, 90,000 people stayed for 10 hours. Baez used a considerable portion of her singing time for a speech appealing to the youth: "The only way the government will ever change is if we force them to change. And that's now our job."

Six days later, on June 12, Baez sang and spoke to an anti-nuclear rally in New York's Central Park, the largest demonstration since the Vietnam War days. Nearly a million people attended. Then she flew off to tour Japan once more.

In Paris, on July 15, 1983, Baez performed to a throng of more than 100,000 at the Place de la Concorde, the site of the French Revolution, and dedicated her songs to change through non-violence. In September, she sang at an open-air concert in Würzburg, Germany. The young people who came to hear her were impressed by more than her beautiful voice. They commented on how she talked with them, not at them, and seemed to care about them.

In 1984, Baez amazed everyone by agreeing to tour again with Dylan and Carlos Santana. Because of their long friendship, Baez signed no official contract with her "blood brother." In Copenhagen, she decided to leave the tour and fly to Italy for a hastily assembled tour of her own.

The new year of 1985 brought some happy moments with old friends at a three-day reunion in Boston's Symphony Hall for those who had sung at Club 47 in Harvard Square. That same summer,

"Good morning, children of the eighties! This is your Woodstock!" shouted Baez, the first performer at Live Aid in Philadelphia in 1985. One of only four artists to play both Woodstock and Live Aid, Baez kicked off the all-day transcontinental affair with a rendition of "Amazing Grace."

Baez attended a Newport festival reunion, celebrating the day, 26 years earlier, that had changed her life.

The following fall, Baez and Amnesty's Ginetta Sagan visited Lech Walesa, leader of Solidarity, the union movement in Poland. By then, Baez seemed to have come to terms with many difficult situations. Her son, Gabe, had gone to live with his father. David Harris had remarried when Gabriel was 12, and Baez had felt that her son needed the firm hand of a man and a family life.

On the road Baez continued to blend fun with work—finding new loves but always returning to her solitude. Between her many trips, she managed to go home to her peaceful Carmel Valley and write her autobiography.

The 1985 Live Aid concert had ushered in a new era of "political pop," the protest music of the 1980s. It was Amnesty International that inspired the revival in protest music. Amnesty had become convinced that pop culture could help raise funds. Its 25th anniversary concert in 1986 and the Conspiracy of Hope tour that followed brought money and new members into the human rights organization and further changed the face of rock 'n' roll.

During the Conspiracy of Hope tour, Baez shared the limelight with the Irish group U2, which for years had performed songs about their politically troubled homeland; the power trio the Police, a British band that featured bassist, lead singer, and composer, Sting, who had recently become active in human rights and environmental causes; a released South African political prisoner and singer named Fela Kuti, and Dylan. The tour spearheaded the new protest revival. The rock singers began to enjoy the kind of camaraderie that folksingers had in the 1960s. Following the tour, many recording artists performed political songs at their concerts.

On July 11, 1988, London's Wembley Stadium was the site of the Nelson Mandela 70th Birthday Tribute. For 11 hours, a live audience of 72,000 and hundreds of millions more people glued to their television sets in 63 countries heard reggae artists, rappers, soul singers, rock bands, and of course, Joan Baez. Nelson Mandela, a lawyer and the political leader of South Africa's oppressed black majority, had been in jail for much of his adult life. The all-white South African government had imprisoned Mandela for his political activities. Though one purpose of the concert was to call for Mandela's freedom, the black leader remained in jail. Still, as a result of the birthday celebration, people who had never heard about South Africa, its apartheid government, or Mandela moved

Joan Baez in her San Francisco home. Not content to rest on her laurels, Baez continues to record and perform and remains committed to social causes. Her passion for nonviolence, human and civil rights, and music remains as strong today as it ever was.

to support his campaign to end racist policies in South Africa. In 1990, Mandela was finally freed by the South African government, and talks aimed at abolishing apartheid began.

By 1990, Baez had achieved a personal and professional balance. Through all of the ups and downs of more than three decades, the once shy and nervous girl who had flinched when she was called a "dirty Mexican" had emerged triumphant. In 1968, *Rolling Stone* magazine had called Baez "a woman of international stature whose every movement, thought and gesture authenticated inseparable commitments to her art and to nonviolence." As she was then, she is today.

Discography

1960	*Joan Baez*	Vanguard
1960	*Folk Festival at Newport '59*	Vanguard
1961	*Joan Baez Volume 2*	Vanguard
1962	*Joan Baez in Concert*	Vanguard
1963	*Joan Baez in Concert Part 2*	Vanguard
1964	*Joan Baez 5*	Vanguard
1965	*Farewell, Angelina*	Vanguard
1966	*Nöel*	Vanguard
1967	*Joan*	Vanguard
1968	*Baptism: A Journey Through Our Time*	Vanguard
1968	*Any Day Now*	Vanguard
1969	*David's Album*	Vanguard
1969	*One Day at a Time*	Vanguard
1970	*Joan Baez—The First Ten Years*	Vanguard

1970	*Woodstock*	Cotillion
1971	*Blessed Are . . .*	Vanguard
1972	*Big Sur Folk Festival*	Columbia
1972	*Come from the Shadows*	A & M
1973	*Hits/Greatest & Others*	Vanguard
1973	*Where Are You Now, My Son?*	A & M
1974	*Gracias a la Vida*	A & M
1974	*Contemporary Ballad Book*	Vanguard
1975	*Diamonds and Rust*	A & M
1976	*From Every Stage*	A & M
1976	*Gulf Winds*	A & M
1976	*Love Song Album*	Vanguard
1977	*Blowin' Away*	Portrait
1977	*Best of Joan C. Baez*	A & M
1979	*Honest Lullaby*	Portrait
1980	*Joan Baez—European Tour*	Portrait
1989	*Diamonds and Rust in the Bull Ring*	Gold Castle
1989	*Speaking of Dreams*	Gold Castle

Chronology

Jan. 9, 1941	Born Joan Chandros Baez in Staten Island, New York
1950–51	Lives in Baghdad, Iraq, with family
1959	Performs at Club 47 and coffeehouses in Cambridge, Massachusetts; appears at Newport Folk Festival in July
1960	Records first album; tours colleges and concert halls; Carnegie Hall debut
1961	Meets Bob Dylan at Gerde's Folk City in New York
Nov. 23, 1962	*Time* magazine cover story
1963	Performs with Bob Dylan at March on Washington; appears with Lyndon B. Johnson at White House presidential gala
1964	Tours with Dylan in the spring; joins Martin Luther King's Selma-to-Montgomery march; Berkeley Free Speech Movement sit-in
1965	Founds, with Ira Sandperl, Institute for the Study of Nonviolence; Johnson escalates the war in Vietnam; Baez performs at first demonstration in Washington against the Vietnam War; tours London with Dylan

1967	Arrested for civil disobedience
1968	Marries David Victor Harris
1969	Harris goes to prison for draft resistance; Baez plays at Woodstock festival; birth of son, Gabriel Earl Harris
1971	Harris is released; Baez and Harris write *Coming Out*
1972	Baez and Harris separate; Baez founds Amnesty International West Coast; visits North Vietnam during U.S. bombings
1973	Divorces Harris
1978	Tours Soviet Union, visits with dissidents Andrei Sakharov and Elena Bonner
1980	Sings at memorial service for Salvadoran archbishop Oscar Romero; tours extensively in Latin America
1982	Appears at nuclear freeze demonstrations in New York and California
1984	Tours with Dylan and Carlos Santana in Europe
1985	Performs at Live Aid concert; meets with Solidarity leader Lech Walesa in Poland
1987	Autobiography *And a Voice to Sing With* is published
July 1988	Performs at the Nelson Mandela 70th Birthday Tribute in London

Further Reading

Baez, Joan. *And a Voice to Sing With: A Memoir.* New York: Summit Books, 1987.

Denselow, Robin. *When the Music's Over: The Story of Political Pop.* London: Faber & Faber, 1989.

Didion, Joan. *Slouching Towards Bethlehem.* New York: Farrar, Straus & Giroux, 1961.

Draper, Hal. *Berkeley: The New Student Revolt.* New York: Grove Press, 1965.

Dunaway, David King. *How Can I Keep from Singing: Pete Seeger.* New York: McGraw-Hill, 1989.

Halstead, Fred. *Out Now! A Participant's Account of the American Movement Against the Vietnam War.* New York: Monad Press, 1978.

Harris, David, and Joan Baez-Harris. *Coming Out.* New York: Pocket Books, 1971.

Rorabaugh, W. J. *Berkeley at War: The 1960s.* New York: Oxford University Press, 1989.

Scaduto, Anthony. *Bob Dylan.* New York: Grosset & Dunlap, 1971.

Shelton, Robert. *No Direction Home: The Life and Music of Bob Dylan.* New York: Morrow, 1986.

Spitz, Bob. *Dylan, A Biography.* New York: McGraw-Hill, 1989.

Zinn, Howard. *A People's History of the United States.* New York: Harper & Row, 1980.

Index

HEDDA GARZA lives in Upstate New York where she works as a free-lance writer, editor, and lecturer. Her articles on Hispanic history and culture have appeared in many newspapers and national magazines. She is also the author of *Salvador Allende* and *Francisco Franco* in the Chelsea House series WORLD LEADERS—PAST & PRESENT.

RODOLFO CARDONA is professor of Spanish and comparative literature at Boston University. A renowned scholar, he has written many works of criticism, including *Ramon, a Study of Gomez de la Serna and His Works* and *Visión del esperpento: Teoría y práctica del esperpento en Valle-Inclan*. Born in San José, Costa Rica, he earned his B.A. and M.A. from Louisiana State University and received a Ph.D. from the University of Washington. He has taught at Case Western Reserve University, the University of Pittsburgh, the University of Texas at Austin, the University of New Mexico, and Harvard University.

JAMES COCKCROFT is currently a visiting professor of Latin American and Caribbean studies at the State University of New York at Albany. A three-time Fulbright scholar, he earned a Ph.D. from Stanford University and has taught at the University of Massachusetts, the University of Vermont, and the University of Connecticut. He is the author or coauthor of numerous books on Latin American subjects, including *Neighbors in Turmoil: Latin America, The Hispanic Experience in the United States: Contemporary Issues and Perspectives,* and *Outlaws in the Promised Land: Mexican Immigrant Workers and America's Future.*